When
FOOTBALL *Was*
FOOTBALL

SOUTHAMPTON

First published in 2012

A catalogue record for this book is available from the British Library

ISBN: 978-0-857331-81-6

Published by Haynes Publishing, Sparkford, Yeovil,
Somerset BA22 7JJ, UK
Tel: 01963 442030 Fax: 01963 440001
Int. tel: +44 1963 442030 Int. fax: +44 1963 440001
E-mail: sales@haynes.co.uk
Website: www.haynes.co.uk

Haynes North America Inc., 861 Lawrence Drive,
Newbury Park, California 91320, USA

Images © Mirrorpix

Creative Director: Kevin Gardner
Designed for Haynes by BrainWave

Printed and bound in the US

When
FOOTBALL *Was*
FOOTBALL

SOUTHAMPTON

A Nostalgic Look at a Century of the Club

David James

Contents

Foreword

I am immensely proud of what I achieved at Southampton when I took over from the legendary Ted Bates as manager in July 1973. That great day at Wembley on 1st May 1976 when we lifted the cup against all the odds, promotion back to the flight in 1978, the brilliant League Cup run of 1979 where Cloughie's Forest denied us in an epic Wembley final, and the 1983–84 season – when we ran the mighty Liverpool all the way for the title and were cruelly denied in the FA Cup semi-final by Everton – are all cherished memories.

Through almost all of Southampton's rich history, the *Mirror* and its sister papers have been there to report on the great games, the famous players, the brilliant results and, as well, the heartbreaks.

The evocative pictures in this book make those events and characters come to life: the FA Cup successes, promotions, unforgettable European nights at The Dell, and legends such as Charlie Wayman, Terry Paine, Ron Davies, Mick Channon, Peter Shilton, Kevin Keegan, Alan Shearer, the Wallace brothers, Matthew Le Tissier and, of course, Mr Southampton himself, the late, great Ted Bates.

This book also serves as a reminder that there's something special and unique about Southampton FC. We may not have had the financial muscle of the big boys, but down the years we have consistently punched above our

weight, managed to attract some of the biggest names in the game and also produced our fair share of England internationals.

The 1970s and early 1980s were, without doubt, glorious days and, despite administration and two relegations, Southampton is still a well-supported club, underpinned by core family values which have been rewarded by promotion back to the Premier League.

This is a celebration of a golden age for football, and a fine portrait of a wonderful club.

Lawrie McMenemy MBE

Saints Alive
1885-1939

When Southampton boss Tom Parker signed 19-year-old Edric Thornton Bates on 3rd May 1937 little did he know it would turn out to be a defining moment in the club's history. Ted, as he would become known in the game, played for Saints as a man and boy, and then led the club into the top flight for the first time ever as manager.

The early 1900s were a great success, and some of the finest talent in the country was lured to The Dell, but it was Edric Thornton Bates who really brought this great club to life and, in doing so, made history.

> "What Ted did for Southampton, with next to no money, is equal to what Matt Busby and Bill Shankly did for their clubs. He also did it with his feet on the ground.
>
> Terry Paine

Ted Bates settles into his Dell surroundings in the late 1930s. They were surroundings that he became extremely comfortable with, both as a player and manager, earning the nickname "Mr Southampton". He was also honoured with an MBE later in his career.

November 1885: Club is founded by members of the St Mary's Church of England Young Men's Association. The first match is against Freemantle, their main rivals, and the kit is white with a red sash, something Saints would wear to commemorate the club's 125th anniversary in 2010. **1887–88:** Beat Southampton Harriers 2-1 in a replay to win the Hampshire Junior Cup. **1888–89:** Win Hampshire Junior Cup again, beating Christchurch 3-0 at Bar End in Winchester. **1889–90:** Win Hampshire Junior Cup for third successive year and keep the trophy. The biggest crowd to watch a game in Hampshire sees the Saints win 3-0 over Lymington. Gate receipts of £51 are recorded. **1890–91:** Beat Royal Engineers 3-1 in the Hampshire Senior Cup final in front of an estimated crowd of 4,000. **1891–92:** Expelled from the FA Cup in the first year of entry for fielding ineligible players. Crowned Hampshire Senior Cup champions. **1892–93:** Beaten 2-1 by Freemantle in front of 7,000 fans in the Hampshire Senior Cup final at the County Ground. But an 8-0 hammering by First Division Stoke in a prestige end-of-season friendly underlines the gulf in class between non-league clubs and those at the top table of English football.

How the Mirror Covered Saints in the Early Years

By the time the *Mirror* launched in November 1903, Southampton had established themselves as one of the biggest sides in the south with two FA Cup final appearances – albeit both defeats – and several Southern League titles.

They had put themselves on the map and were beginning to draw decent-sized crowds as football enjoyed a boom in popularity up and down the country.

The FA Cup quarter-final replay clash with Everton on 11th March 1908 drew 21,690 to The Dell after 40,000 had seen the 0-0 draw at Goodison. The first pictures of the Saints in action in the *Mirror* are of this match.

ABOVE: Southampton's first ever mention in the *Daily Mirror* sports pages was a 1-0 defeat to Tottenham Hotspur in the Western League on 29th December 1903. It is a far cry from the column inches sport is given today. The match got two lines at the foot of page 5 under the inauspicious heading of "Miscellaneous Sport".

Caption (centre photographs):

SOUTHAMPTON DEFEAT EVERTON IN THE REPLAYED CUP-TIE AT SOUTHAMPTON YESTERDAY.

Last Saturday Southampton visited Liverpool, and played a drawn game against Everton in the fourth round of the English Cup, no goals being scored. Yesterday they were victorious in the replay at Southampton by three goals to two. (1) The first goal to Southampton. (2) A near shave for Everton: a Southampton forward shoots wide. (3) The Everton back saves the situation.—("Daily Mirror" photographs.)

1894–95: Join Southern League and reach FA Cup first round for the first time, but are beaten 4-1 by Nottingham Forest. **1895–96:** Southampton St Mary's causes a massive uproar by poaching some of the biggest stars in the Football League. Southern League clubs are unrestricted by the maximum wage cap imposed by the Football League so are able to offer more money. **1896–97:** Win the Southern League title, going the whole season undefeated. Captain Jack Farrell scores 13 goals in 20 appearances. **1897–98:** Become a limited company, changing their name to Southampton Football Club. A share issue of £5,000 is earmarked for the acquisition of a new ground. **March 1898:** Saints become first Southern League side to reach the FA Cup semi-finals but lose 2-0 to Nottingham Forest in a replay at Crystal Palace. **May 1898:** Win Southern League. **1898–99:** Move to a newly built ground called The Dell at a cost of £10,000, but have to initially rent the stadium. The Saints did, though, take ownership of the ground in the early part of the 20th century and it would pave the way for their 103-year stay. **September 1898:** Beat Brighton 4-1 in the first match at The Dell in front of a crowd of 6,524, only a third of its potential 25,000 capacity. Watty Keay scores the first goal. **April 1899:** Southern League champions for third successive year.

March 30, 1908.   THE DAILY MIRROR.   Page 11.

NEWCASTLE UNITED AND WOLVERHAMPTON WANDERERS REACH THE FINAL.

Southampton gave a very disappointing exhibition against Wolverhampton Wanderers at Stamford Bridge on Saturday, the Wanderers winning by 2 goals to nil. (1) Lunn, the Wolverhampton goalkeeper, making a good save. (2) Wolverhampton's second goal—Burrows fails to save. (3) Pedley, the Wolverhampton outside left, avoids the attention of the Southampton backs. (4) Harrison, the Wolverhampton outside right, who was chiefly responsible for the two goals obtained by his side, carries away the ball as a memento of the match.—("Daily Mirror" photographs.)

Fulham were overwhelmed by Newcastle United in the semi-final tie for the English Cup at Liverpool on Saturday, being defeated by 6 goals to nil. (1) Skene, the Fulham goalkeeper, taking the ball from the toe of a Newcastle forward. (2) Police officers controlling the huge crush at one corner of the ground. (3) Skene punching out. (4 and 5) Newcastle score two of their goals.—("Daily Mirror" photographs.)

CAMBRIDGE BEATS OXFORD BY SIX EVENTS TO FOUR AT QUEEN'S CLUB.

The inter-University sports at Queen's Club on Saturday resulted in a win for the Cambridge men by 6 events to 4. (1) The hurdle race—(A) K. Powell (Cambridge), winner, beats (B) E. R. J. Hussey, second. (2) T. H. Just (Cambridge) winning the half-mile in 1m. 58 4-5s. (3) The start for the mile—C. Howard-Smith falls. (4) A. C. Bollerby (Cambridge) wins the high jump—5ft. 8in.—("Daily Mirror" photographs.)

SOUTHERN LEAGUE FORM.

Southampton's Sweet Revenge on the 'Spurs.

By F. B. WILSON (Cambridge University).

Yesterday's play in both Southern and Western Leagues upset all calculations and conclusions drawn from a careful study of the teams at work. Following their heavy defeat in the Western League at the hands of the 'Spurs on Saturday, a defeat of five goals to love, Southampton turned the tables on their old opponents yesterday at the Dell, and just managed to win by one goal to nil.

* * *

This was in the Southern League, and it will be noted that the 'Spurs' failure to annex the points leaves Fulham in a very strong position at the head of the table. Then the Fulham men, after the doughty deeds they have been doing during the last week or so, went down in the Western League before Brentford, at Brentford, a team which only stands eighth on the Southern League list.

* * *

Brighton and Hove Albion won from Watford at Brighton by 2 to none, their first victory for some time, and one which lifts them from the bottom of the League and leaves Watford in that unenviable position. Reading and Queen's Park Rangers drew at Park Royal in the Western branch. Luton, as was to be expected, beat Northampton 1st Luton, in the Southern tournament. Portsmouth and West Ham drew at Portsmouth in the Western League, and Swindon beat Millwall at North Greenwich in a friendly.

* * *

The great match of the day was, of course, that between the Saints and the 'Spurs at Southampton in the Southern League. Southampton were without Hedley and Harrison, and the 'Spurs were heavily handicapped by the absence of V. J. Woodward and "Sandy" Tait. Both sides were on their mettle, and a very even first half was fought out at a tremendous pace. Brown put his side ahead, after some clever work, amidst a scene of great enthusiasm.

The crowd, which numbered about 15,000 spectators, was kept on the tip-toe of excitement right to the finish. The 'Spurs made unceasing efforts to equalise, and twice it seemed as though Kyle, with practically an open goal, must get through. Untiring work by the backs, however, and brilliant goalkeeping by Chewley kept the home goal intact, and when the last whistle sounded Southampton were still leading by 1 goal to nil.

LEFT: Saints get sweet revenge on Spurs with a 1-0 win in front of an estimated 15,000 at The Dell. They had been beaten 5-0 by the London side in the Western League just days before.

Chasing Their Shadows!   See Page 11.

The Daily Mirror

SECOND ROUND OF THE CUP: KEEN BATTLES AND LOW SCORES: FIVE GAMES DRAWN

ABOVE: The *Mirror* says it all as Saints fall apart in the 2-0 FA Cup semi-final, and are defeated by Wolves at Stamford Bridge in March 1908.

RIGHT: A 1-1 draw with Cardiff in the FA Cup second round at The Dell makes back-page news (top right).

LEFT: How the *Mirror* reported Saints winning the Third Division (South) title with a 5-0 win over Newport at The Dell in May 1922.

April 1900: Hammered 4-0 in the FA Cup final by Bury at Crystal Palace in front of a crowd of 68,945. **1901:** Southern League champions with Edgar Chadwick (14) and Alf Milward (12) top goalscorers. **December 1901:** Albert Brown scores seven goals as Saints thrash Northampton 11-0 at The Dell. Brown went on to score 25 goals in 25 games. **April 1902:** Beaten 2-1 in FA Cup final replay by Sheffield United. Harry Wood had scored in the first game for Saints in the 1-1 draw. **1902–03:** Fred Harrison scores 17 goals in 13 games including five-goal hauls against Wellingborough and Northampton. Watford are hammered 11-0 at The Dell in December and Saints are crowned Southern champions. **1903–04:** Win Southern League for the sixth time in 10 seasons with Harrison scoring 27 goals in 32 appearances. **1920–21:** Join newly formed Football League Third Division. Bill Rawlings hits 18 goals and Saints finish the season as runners-up to Crystal Palace – but only the champions are promoted. **1921–22:** League is split into North and South sections and Saints are the first champions of Third Division (South). Bill Rawlings scores 30 league goals. **1929:** The East Stand of The Dell is destroyed by fire after the 3-0 win over Swansea on 4th May 1929.

—LEGENDS—

Harry Wood

Nicknamed the Wolf, Wood captained Saints for seven seasons during one of their most successful eras, winning the Southern League four times.

Wood was an ever-present player in his first season, making 24 appearances and scoring 16 goals as Saints took the Southern League title for the third time.

In his final season, the gate money for Woods' testimonial against Aston Villa totalled £106 5s 6d and was boosted by donations from the public to make a total benefit cheque of £250 5s.

Southampton are slowly but surely coming back to form. For the last week or two their veteran forward. "Harry" Wood, who is probably the oldest player in first-class League football, has been turning out again for the "Saints," and his presence has worked wonders. He led up to the first goal scored by Hedley at Northampton on Saturday. This won the match, as although Southampton obtained two more goals, one by Hedley and one from a penalty, the first goal was the important one, as although they played well, the Northampton forwards could make no impression on the Southampton defence, which was worthy of the champions, Molyneux, Lee, and Clawley being particularly conspicuous.

POSITIONS OF THE CLUBS.

	Played	Won	Lost	Drn	For	Agst	Pts
Bristol R. (3)	14	7	3	3	25	11	17
Reading (6)	11	7	2	2	22	16	16
Southampton (1)	12	6	2	4	20	14	16
W. Ham U. (12)	12	5	3	4	17	10	15
Queen's Pk. R. (5)	12	5	3	4	19	13	13
Northampton (15)	12	5	3	4	12	11	12
Portsmouth (4)	10	4	3	0	26	21	12
Plymouth A. (9)	11	4	3	2	19	12	12
N. Brompton (16)	11	4	3	4	17	14	12
Tottenham H. (2)	11	4	3	3	10	11	11
Fulham (11)	12	3	4	5	9	11	11
Brentford (13)	12	4	6	2	15	15	10
Watford	12	4	5	1	10	8	9
....ighton (17)	10	3	4	3	15	9	9
....llwall (7)	13	3	7	3	10	20	9
Swindon T. (10)	12	3	6	3	15	22	9
...uton (8)	12	2	6	4	9	21	8
Wellingboro (14)	9	1	8	0		30	

"SIGNING-ON" NOTES.

Football Clubs and Their Players— Some of the Changes.

It is understood that Harry Wood's long and honourable career with the Southampton club is about to terminate, and that the old "Wolf" has been engaged by the Portsmouth Club in the capacity of coach.

Stevenson, the Millwall back, is not expected to sign on again for his old club.

Only Mellors, White, and Hulme, of the Brighton and Hove Albion, have been retained.

Plymouth Argyle have signed on of their old players: Sutcliffe and Horne (goalkeepers); Saul (back); Leech and C. Clark (half-backs); Buck, Owens, Wright, and Jack (forwards). The players leaving, all of whom will more than likely be seen with First League clubs, either English or Scotch, are Robinson (goal); Ashby and A. Clark (backs); Banks (half-back); Cocks, McLuckie, Dalrymple, Picken, Hodgkinson, and Chadburn (forwards).

Portsmouth have retained Buick, Walker, Harris, Bowman, S. Smith, W. Smith, Lee, Halliday, Digweed, and a few other local men. Corbin, a promising young forward whom Sheffield Wednesday and Southampton were after, has been bought out of the Royal Marine Artillery. Cunliffe is also expected to sign. Thompson, Young, Campbell, McDonald, Axford, and several others will probably go elsewhere.

William Ford, one of Portsmouth's forwards, has been transferred to West Ham.

The Woolwich Arsenal F.C. directors secured the signatures of two more of their old players on Saturday, Badger and Cross, having decided to remain at Plumstead.

Sheffield United F.C. have notified that Foulkes, the famous heavy-weight goalkeeper, will not be retained. Harry Mitchell, a capital outside right-winger, who has figured for Barrow Hill, an East Derbyshire club, has signed on for the club.

At Southampton on Saturday evening Clawley and Houlker signed for another season. Fraser, it is stated, intends to return to Scotland.

ABOVE: The *Mirror* reveals that legend Harry Wood is to join Portsmouth as a coach in May 1905.

LEFT: The *Mirror's* story is confirmed as Harry Wood joins Pompey.

FOOTBALL —STATS—

Harry Wood

Name: Harry Wood

Date of Birth: 26th June 1868

Died: July 1951 (aged 83)

Position: Inside-forward

Playing Career: Wolves, Southampton (1898–1905)

Southampton Appearances: 158

Southampton Goals: 62

England Caps: 3

....rtsmouth have secured the services of R. Jackson (left ..), T Stewart (full-back), both of Sunderland, and ....e also re-engaged Cunliffe. Cooper, of Wellingborough, ...well as Harry Wood, of Southampton, have been ...aged as trainers. Jackson has been seven years with ...derland, and for two seasons captained the team. ... has also played for the North against the South. ...wart is a youngster who has just completed his first ...son in League football. Other signatures are ex-...ted.

—LEGENDS—

Bill Rawlings

Second on the club's list of all-time goalscorers, Rawlings starred in the Southern League and then the Football League for Saints. In March 1928 he signed for Manchester United, scoring on his debut. Port Vale paid a four-figure fee for his services in November 1929, but he suffered a serious ankle injury on Christmas Day 1929

FOOTBALL —STATS—

Bill Rawlings

Name: Bill Rawlings

Date of Birth: 3rd January 1896

Died: September 1972 (aged 76)

Position: Centre-forward

Playing Career: Southampton (1918–28), Man Utd, Port Vale

Southampton Appearances: 327

Southampton Goals: 175

England Caps: 2

during a 2-1 home defeat by Stockport. He had recovered by the spring of 1930, but was unable to return to the first team. Rawlings also won two England caps.

LEFT: Bill Rawlings is pictured on the back of the *Mirror* (bottom row, middle) challenging Carter of West Ham during their 1-1 FA Cup draw at The Dell in March 1923. Rawlings was Southampton's goalscorer.

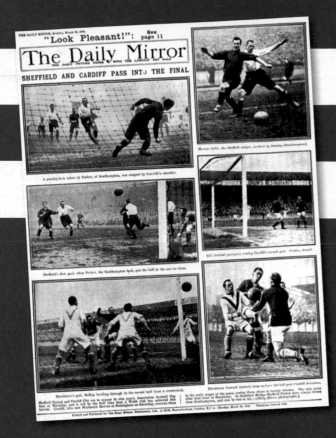

LEFT: Southampton's 2-0 defeat to Sheffield United in the FA Cup at Stamford Bridge shared the back page with the other last-four tie in which Cardiff beat Blackburn in March 1925.

RIGHT: Again Saints fall at the semi-final hurdle. This time it's a 2-1 defeat to Arsenal in 1927.

Tourism from America collapsed as the Great Depression took hold on both sides of the Atlantic in the 1930s. Southampton docks, for so long the lifeblood of the city, was badly hit and many workers were laid off. The knock-on effect was felt by the football club and they were plunged into financial meltdown. The *Mirror* reported that the directors were so concerned about the future that they set up a £1,000 fighting fund to keep the club going – and, furthermore, the economic problems coincided with one of the bleakest periods in Southampton's history. They crashed to their heaviest ever defeat – an 8-0 thrashing by Tottenham at White Hart Lane in 1936 – as relegation battles became commonplace. The one significant signing during that period was that of one Ted Bates from Norwich on his 19th birthday in November 1937. It would begin Bates' astonishing 66-year association with the club.

Uncertain Times

Ted Drake (left), pictured with Alex James, in 1936, two years after his move to Arsenal from Southampton.

The Gunners had coveted Drake long before they finally got their man, after some scintillating performances and brilliant goalscoring feats for Southampton.

Drake announced his arrival from Winchester City at The Dell in June 1931 in some style. He scored 20 goals in the 1932–33 season, which first attracted the attention of Arsenal boss Herbert Chapman – but Drake turned down a move to Highbury.

However, Arsenal, with George Allison now in charge, renewed their interest and Drake finally joined the Gunners for £6,500 in March 1934 as Saints were forced to balance their books.

Drake made 74 appearances for Southampton, scoring 48 goals.

With his family and fiancée Miss Ruby Maggs, Ted Drake packs his boots and his bag after his transfer from Southampton to Arsenal.

Roaring Forties
1939-1954

Manager Bill Dodgin talks tactics with his players in March 1949 on the scaled-down Dell pitch – one inch to one yard – that was installed in the home dressing room. It's a far cry from the technology that is available to league clubs nowadays.

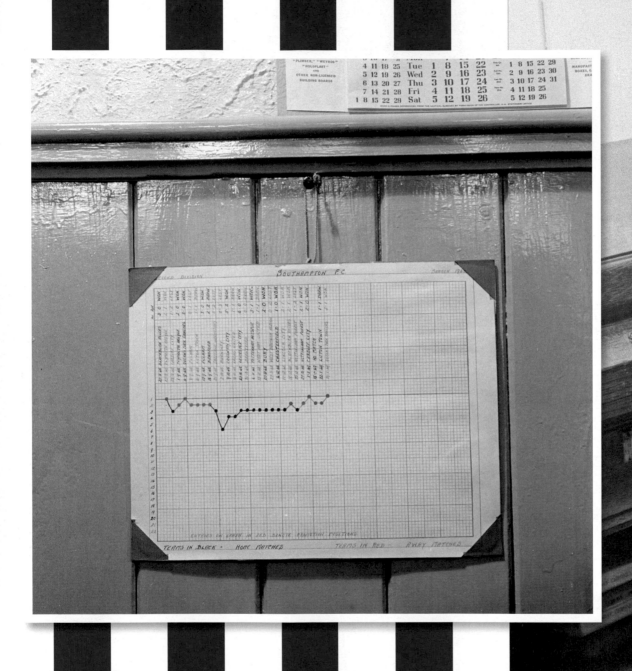

RIGHT: Bill Dodgin goes through the laborious task of charting Southampton's progress through the 1948–49 season. They finished third in the Second Division, two points behind champions Fulham, after a poor run-in that saw them collect just five points from their last seven games.

The War Years

Firefighters in Southampton do their best to contain the smouldering remains as another Nazi air raid in 1943 causes utter devastation through the city.

Just as the 1939–40 season got under way, the Second World War broke out and all games were suspended. Many clubs continued to play friendly games and Saints were one of them. But they were forced to play away from The Dell for almost three months as the area had been designated "unsafe" due to the production of arms.

No sooner had matches returned to Southampton than a bomb landed on The Dell pitch in November 1940 and opened up an 18-foot crater, damaging an underground culvert and flooding the pitch. In consequence, Saints switched their home games to Fratton Park for a brief period.

The City of Southampton was badly hit by Nazi attacks and targeted with large-scale air raids in the first phase of the Blitz. The port also became a specific strategic target.

There were 57 attacks and the Air Raid Precautions Department reported that over 2,000 bombs and 30,000 incendiary devices were dropped on the city. The High Street was flattened and Southampton could be seen burning from as far away as Cherbourg in France.

SOUTHAMPTON PROCLAIMS: WE FIGHT ON

FROM OUR SPECIAL CORRESPONDENT

Southampton, Tuesday.

A proclamation to the people of Southampton calling on them to continue their part in waging the battle of Britain was issued today from the bomb scarred civic centre.

It is being posted all over the city and in the hamlets and townships surrounding and is headed boldly in big block letters:

"PEOPLE OF SOUTHAMPTON"

It reads: "Although the town has been severely damaged it has not suffered any permanent injury. Some of the public services are temporarily interrupted, but the necessary repairs will be quickly carried out and the services will be in operation again in a few days' time.

"Everybody should get in touch with his employer or the nearest Labour Exchange in order to resume his work.

"The battle of Britain must go on. All Southampton must continue to play its vital part."

The notice, issued by the Ministry of Information, is signed by Mr. Harold Butler, Regional Commissioner for the southern region, and the Mayor of Southampton.

Reply Is: "Rebuild"

For many thousands of the people this notice merely advertises a situation which they can see with their own eyes.

They are still in their homes and there they intend to stay.

Their food arrives almost as usual. It may be a bit late, it may come from a strange shop, but it is there. No red tape is being allowed to hold people back from a single meal, and a similar understanding is being shown towards those in need of financial help.

Hustle is the keynote of the work of making things shipshape municipally and domestically, and today the directors of one blitzed business concern at least met in a local hotel and decided to put rebuilding plans in hand within a week.

Camping Out

In scores of damaged houses remnants of jagged glass are being knocked out of window frames, holes boarded over, rooms swept clean of soot and rubble and bomb fragments, and an approach to normal life sought.

But a new night life has come to Southampton now. For many families are using their homes only during the day and are camping out at night.

In one strip of wooded country only a few miles from the city centre several hundred people are sleeping under the trees. They manage to pass a tolerable night.

The custodian of this strip of woodland told me that the people come on bicycles and on foot, many of them pushing their children in prams. He lets them all come—barring only the wealthier people in cars. They must go farther afield.

In the morning they all go back to their posts in the battle of Britain.

The people of Southampton defiantly hit back at the Germans in the *Mirror*, despite the devastation their bombing raids caused across the city.

Sir Alf Ramsey, who played for Southampton between 1943 and 1949, gets in some practice at The Dell. He made 90 league appearances in his six years at Saints after signing from Portsmouth. Ramsey was knighted in 1967 after he had led England to World Cup glory.

December 1945: Doug McGibbon bags six goals in the 7-0 win over Chelsea at The Dell. His first goal comes after just four seconds, the club's quickest ever strike. **1947–48:** Saints miss out on promotion after finishing third in the Second Division. Charlie Wayman hits 17 league goals. **June 1948:** Southampton tour Brazil. It takes 12 days at sea to reach Rio. Sir Alf Ramsey joins the squad by plane after winning an England B cap against Switzerland. They lose 2-1 to giants Vasco da Gama in the final game of the tour – but Ramsey said it was "one of the best matches in which I've played".

"Charlie was a God in Southampton and a wonderful player. I wandered around the town and there were reminders of how popular he was everywhere. I could never replace him."

Eddie Brown, who came from Preston as Wayman headed for Deepdale

Despite spending only three years at The Dell, the prolific Charlie Wayman established himself as a legend in the late 1940s.

WAYMAN TELLS: WHY I AM RESOLVED TO GO

By CHARLES WAYMAN
(Newcastle United centre forward)

I AM a 100 per cent. Newcastle fan. So was my father.

But I am determined to leave the club now.

The directors will consider my request for a transfer today. They may grant it. They may, on the other hand, ask me to come back into the team.

LET ME SAY JUST THIS. I STILL WANT TO GO. BUT IF THEY DO PUT ME IN THE TEAM IN THE MEANWHILE I SHALL CONTINUE TO DO MY VERY BEST.

I always have done. I always shall do. I give my word on that. Whatever the team I play in I shall try my hardest because I could not in my heart do anything else.

The decision to keep me out of the semi-final side upset me. It still does. I feel that whatever happens, I must leave the club.

I was banking on playing in every game this season. It was my big ambition, and there wasn't much longer to go. That is over now.

What gets me down still more are the rumours in my home town that I was dropped because I had been drinking, and because I fought with Len Shackleton.

BOTH THESE STORIES ARE WITHOUT ANY FOUNDATION AT ALL. I AM TEE-TOTAL. I WOULD NOT BE SUCH A FOOL AS TO START DRINKING WITH MY FOOTBALL CAREER IN FRONT OF ME.

And I am on the best of personal terms with Shack.

People believed all this nonsense because they could see no other reason why I should be so suddenly dropped from the team.

I have denied the stories a thousand times, but people seem to think there is no smoke without fire.

THEY JUST COULDN'T GET IT I HAD BEEN DROPPED BECAUSE I WAS NOT CONSIDERED GOOD ENOUGH FOR THE FIRST TEAM.

I have said that I am on the best possible terms with Shackleton. That is true. But remember this: Shack is a very difficult partner to play with—simply because he is so talented—and it is not always easy to understand what he wants.

Many a time he's called for the ball and I've headed it to him, only to find he's moved into some other position.

I have been criticised, but there isn't much opportunity for picking and choosing when you've got a 6ft. centre-half at your back.

SHACK'S A BRILLIANT FOOTBALLER, AND THERE ARE OTHERS LIKE HIM IN THE NEWCASTLE TEAM.

But I sometimes wonder if it's not better to be in a team where all the players are more or less on the same level, and none of them an outstanding star.

● *Newcastle directors, at their meeting today, will be told that the captain, Joe Harvey, did not report for training yesterday, and that there has been no word from Harvey and Shackleton that they are dissatisfied with their housing conditions.*

Chas. Wayman.

ABOVE: Charlie Wayman writes an emotional first-person piece in the *Mirror* in April 1947 after being dropped by Newcastle for allegedly drinking and fighting with Len Shackleton. In it, he says he is resolved to leave the club.

BELOW: Even back in 1947 it was a race against the clock to secure a signing. With no transfer deals permitted on a Sunday, Southampton signed Charlie Wayman in the nick of time on Saturday night after his train from Newcastle arrived late. Officials whisked him to a hotel and, as he put pen to paper, the chimes rang out for midnight.

WAYMAN SIGNED—THEN CLOCK STRUCK 12

WITH a signed cheque in his pocket, a football manager huddled into his overcoat and anxiously watched the station clock tick towards midnight.

He had decided to exchange £10,000 for the autograph of a stocky little centre-forward who, as an unknown pit-boy, cost only a signing-on fee of £10.

With Sundays banned for transfers, Southampton's William Dodgin knew forms would have to be completed by midnight—or the deal would drag on.

The train in which the player, centre-forward Charles Wayman, was returning to Newcastle from a reserve game was late and when it arrived at ten to twelve United and Southampton officials rushed him across to a hotel, explaining the deal as they went.

"Yes, I'm quite agreeable," said Wayman. Then as the signature was made at a table in the dimly-lit lounge, the cathedral clock chimed the hour.

Bill Dodgin had made his greatest capture—so far in time. The leading goal-scorer in the Second Division last season would in future play for the Saints.

Aberdeen game, Aston Villa's Alex Massie sat alongside David Jack, of Middlesbrough, and representatives of Chelsea and West Bromwich. Player they were all watching was Peter McKennan, Thistle inside right.

Outside the ground Thistle supporters had chalked up on the walls, "We want Peter."

"He had a quiet game, so it looks as though they will keep him."

SCORED AT LAST

BILLY STEEL, Derby County's £15,500 Scottish international inside forward who might just as easily have been a Liverpool player, celebrated his first game at Anfield against the Mersey-

Charles Wayman.

Soccer Sideshow —By NORTHMAN

–LEGENDS–

Charlie Wayman

A prolific centre-forward in the first decade after the Second World War, Wayman was signed by Newcastle from Spennymoor United in 1941 while he was working as a miner. Saints boss Bill Dodgin then snapped him up for £10,000 in October 1947 and he immediately became a Dell favourite. Wayman formed a great partnership with Ted Bates, but left for Preston in 1950 after his wife failed to settle in the area. He continued to score goals at an impressive rate but a knee injury hastened his retirement.

FOOTBALL –STATS–

Charlie Wayman

Name: Charlie Wayman

Date of Birth: 16th May 1922

Died: February 1922 (aged 83)

Position: Striker

Playing Career: Newcastle, Southampton (1947–50), Preston, Middlesbrough, Darlington

Southampton Appearances: 100

Southampton Goals: 73

England Caps: 0

Blowing Promotion

Not even the freezing weather can deter the Saints faithful as they cram into The Dell for the 1-0 win over Barnsley in December 1950; Eddie Brown scores the winner.

Before that, the 1948–49 campaign will be remembered as the one that got away for Southampton. With seven games remaining they were eight points clear at the top of the Second Division but a disastrous run-in – without the injured Charlie Wayman – meant Saints collected just five points from their last seven games and allowed Fulham and West Brom to overtake them. The following season – under Sid McCann who had replaced Bill Dodgin as boss – more heartache followed as Saints missed out again, this time on goal difference.

LEFT: Saints goalkeeper Ian Black is featured as part of the *Mirror*'s brilliant and innovative Magic Feet Series in April 1949. Black is praised for his positioning, agility and braveness. Instead of the usual footprint, the *Mirror* featured his handprints.

BELOW: Saints prepare for their massive promotion clash against West Brom in April 1949 at The Dell with egg and sherry tonics in the dressing room. Such was the importance of the match one Southampton star quipped: "If we lose, we'll walk to the end of the pier – and keep on walking!" The match ended 1-1 but it was the Baggies who were promoted.

Magic Feet—No. 19

The safe hands of Ian Black, Southampton, have played an important part in his club's most successful season.

WHY IS HE A STAR?

Black's anticipation is exceptionally good. He keeps calm, positions himself well, and is agile and daring. Other Southampton defenders play better than they normally would because of their complete confidence in him.

A former motor mechanic, Black joined Southampton from Aberdeen, and has played for Scotland. He is 24, weighs 12st. 7lb., is 6ft. tall.

Here is to add to your collection is his autograph. And as he is a goalkeeper we show you his handprints instead of the usual footprints.

A toast in eggs and sherry 'To victory over Albion'

By JOHN THOMPSON

AFTER two hours of finding fault with each other in their longest-ever tactical talk, Southampton players last night toasted "victory over West Bromwich" in egg and sherry tonics in their dressing room.

Moving coloured discs across a miniature field painted on the floor, they had talked about plans for the most important match in their club's history—the clash today with Albion which can decide the Second Division promotion problem.

Fulham, the other club concerned in the race to the First Division, are at home to Brentford.

Mr. Bill Dodgin, Southampton manager, said: "All the players pooled their ideas after Bill Rochford, our captain, had suggested that everyone should have a say.

"They're so keen to win that they asked for their faults to be discussed so they could try to remedy them."

JACK VERNON, West Bromwich captain.

Wayman Fails to Pass Test.

In a test yesterday Charles Wayman, star centre forward, failed to pass a fitness test.

"Sorry, Bill, it's just not right," he admitted. "In such an important game it's best to field eleven men who are thoroughly fit."

Then he went over to wish good luck to Ted Bates, who will deputise for him.

The Southampton player told me: "If we lose, we'll walk to the end of the pier—and go on walking."

That's how both teams feel about this most critical League match of the season.

West Bromwich stayed the night at Bournemouth. They will not know their teams until just before the kick-off.

Thirteen players had travelled from the Midlands, and four more are to join the party later.

Mr. Jack Smith, West Bromwich manager, said: "We shall have seventeen players at The Dell, but at this moment only five positions have been definitely decided."

Those certain to play are goalkeeper Jim Sanders, right-back Jim Pemberton, centre half Jack Vernon, outside right Billy Elliott, and centre forward Dave Walsh.

No Travelling for Them, so They Start Favourites

Fulham are likely to take both points from Brentford. With only local Derby games to play they have no travelling to do and have a better goal average than either of their rivals.

Although football folk have given them little credit for their success, Fulham start favourites this morning.

Wirss His Deputy Luck

OH, WHAT A SURPRISE FOR THEM!

THREE young pals reported at the Manchester City ground yesterday for instructions about their reserve match today. And all three went home for the shock of their young careers when looked at the notice board. They are all going to make their football League debut together, writes Gerry Loftus.

Outside right, Bill Heans, right half, Ray Gill, and centre forward, Bill Jones, are to play their first senior game together against the Cup finalists, Wolverhampton today. Pals in the reserves the trio hope to field stardom together.

BILL ROCHFORD, Southampton captain.

THE VETERA BOY ARE TH LAST HOPI

LOCAL boy Eddie Brown is studies to become a professional up to lead Preston's attack against Manchester United.

He displaces £5,000 Angus ... buys in their £60,000 spend.

Eddie, one of two hundred ...

> *We worked nicely together. He was a good passer of the ball, Ted. Great footballer and I could fit in with him. I could read him, know where he was going to put the ball.*
>
> Charlie Wayman

Ted Bates takes a training session at The Dell in March 1963.

–LEGENDS– Ted Bates MBE

Bates was a wonderful servant whose finest playing days came between 1947 and 1951 when he formed a great partnership with Charlie Wayman. As manager, he transformed the fortunes of the club, taking Southampton from the Third to the First Division and nurturing some of the finest talent ever seen at The Dell.

FOOTBALL –STATS–

Ted Bates MBE

Name: Ted Bates

Date of Birth: 3rd May 1918

Died: November 2003 (aged 85)

Position: Forward

Playing Career: Norwich, Southampton (1937–53)

Southampton Appearances: 202

Southampton Goals: 63

Managerial Career: Southampton (1955–73)

England Caps: 0

ABOVE: Ted Bates just fails to get on the end of a cross in Southampton's FA Cup defeat at Roker Park in 1951. Sunderland defender Billy Walsh seems unconcerned by Bates' presence.

There's plenty of goalmouth action in the 2-1 win over Blackburn at The Dell in March 1952. However, the early 1950s were not a great period for the club and after several mediocre seasons they were relegated to Third Division (South) in 1953.

Sir Stanley Matthews leaves Saints defender Peter Sillett sprawled on the floor as he gets in a cross during the FA Cup fifth-round clash at The Dell in 1953. The game finished 1-1 and Blackpool won the replay 2-1. The Seasiders went all the way to Wembley and won the cup in the game dubbed the "Matthews Final". Matthews inspired Blackpool to fight back from 3-1 down against Bolton to win 4-3, with Stan Mortensen scoring a hat-trick.

Away from the cup, Saints' league form picked up and Eric Day was scoring for fun. He returned 26 goals in the 1953–54 campaign and went one better the following season when Saints missed out on promotion by two points.

The first team may have been disappointed but the reserves, under Ted Bates and Jimmy Gallagher, won the Football Combination Cup.

> " *You could call it a fairytale the way Ted took us from Division 3 to Division 1 and into Europe but it was commitment and hard work that got him there. He did it with a brilliant youth policy and shrewdness in the transfer market that often bordered on daylight robbery.* "
>
> Terry Paine

Super Ted
1954-1973

Ted Bates prepares his players for an April run-in that included seven league games in 1963. He must have been doing something right as they won five of them to finish fifth in the Second Division.

Ted Bates took over as manager from George Roughton in September 1955 and wasted little time in stamping his authority on the club with a host of signings, including that of Terry Paine, who was being chased by Arsenal.

Paine was immediately thrust into the limelight and made his league debut in March 1957 – a week before his 18th birthday – in the 3-3 draw with Brentford at The Dell.

> " I always felt Terry played the game like he was sitting in the stand. When you're sitting up there, it's easy, isn't it? I played against Finney, Matthews and Shackleton but I think Terry was the most accurate player I ever played with.
>
> George O'Brien "

RIGHT: Eric Day, who played 398 league games for Saints, scoring 145 goals, gave Ted Bates a boost during his first season in charge. Despite a mid-table finish, Day found the target 28 times and was a prolific marksman in his time at The Dell.

BELOW: All eyes are on the ball as Saints threaten in the 1-1 draw at Torquay in November 1957. The 1957–58 season took on extra significance for Ted Bates as the final positions would determine the make-up of the Third and Fourth Divisions now that the regional leagues had been discontinued. Saints finished in the top six – largely thanks to 31 goals from Derek Reeves – to secure their place in the Third Division.

New signing and captain, Cliff Huxford (bending left), and Dick Connor (bending right) are hurdled by Tommy Traynor and George O'Brien during pre-season training in August 1959. It was a fine season, as Saints went on to win the Third Division title.

Ted's Revolution

Saints came alive during the 1959–60 run-in to the season and were crowned champions of the Third Division, with Derek Reeves scoring 39 goals – a Saints record – and new boy George O'Brien, 23.

A major overhaul in the summer of 1959 had seen 14 players leave and nine new faces arrive as Ted Bates began his revolution. Cliff Huxford, from Chelsea, was given the armband and he thrived on the responsibility.

By January, the team had settled and Bates had them playing the Southampton way. First Division Manchester City were thrashed 5-1 at Maine Road in the FA Cup, with Reeves hitting four. His goals were provided by Paine, and Bates described his performance as "the best I've seen from an outside-right".

It provided the impetus for Southampton to go on and win the title.

1959–60 Third Division Top Six

	P	W	D	L	F	A	Pts
Southampton	46	26	9	11	106	75	61
Norwich	46	24	11	11	82	54	59
Shrewsbury	46	18	16	12	97	75	52
Coventry	46	21	10	15	78	63	52
Grimsby	46	18	16	12	87	70	52
Bury	46	21	9	16	64	51	51

RIGHT: Derek Reeves (left) and Terry Paine (right) share a joke in the build-up to the FA Cup fourth-round tie against Watford in 1960.

Ted Bates gave many of the squad their chance after promotion from the Third Division. And it paid off as they finished their first campaign in the Second Division with a comfortable mid-table finish. George O'Brien, here scoring in the FA Cup clash with Watford in 1960, was emerging as a fine marksman alongside Reeves, and his 22 goals topped the charts at The Dell.

The following season O'Brien's stock rose further as he notched 28 goals in a top-six finish.

ABOVE: One fan takes up a particularly precarious position on the wall at the back of the terrace to watch the FA Cup tie with Watford in 1960.

BELOW: Derek Reeves, here putting pressure on the Plymouth defence, continued to make a name for himself with impressive goalscoring feats, none more so than hitting all five in the 5-4 win over Leeds during the League Cup fourth round in December 1960. Incredibly, the game lasted two hours 40 minutes due to two floodlight failures at The Dell.

–LEGENDS–

Derek Reeves

Derek Reeves, who joined Southampton in December 1954, having been demobbed from National Service, and scored on his debut against hometown club, Bournemouth, was the first to benefit from the brilliant Terry Paine and John Sydenham. He was an explosive and lethal finisher and was Saints' top scorer for four consecutive seasons, culminating in 1959–60 when his 39 league goals created not only a club record but a Third Division record which remains to this day.

FOOTBALL –STATS–

Derek Reeves

Name: Derek Reeves

Date of Birth: 27th August 1934

Died: May 1995 (aged 60)

Position: Centre-forward

Playing Career: Southampton (1954–62), Bournemouth

Southampton Appearances: 273

Southampton Goals: 145

England Caps: 0

Derek Reeves is thwarted by the Watford goalkeeper in January 1960.

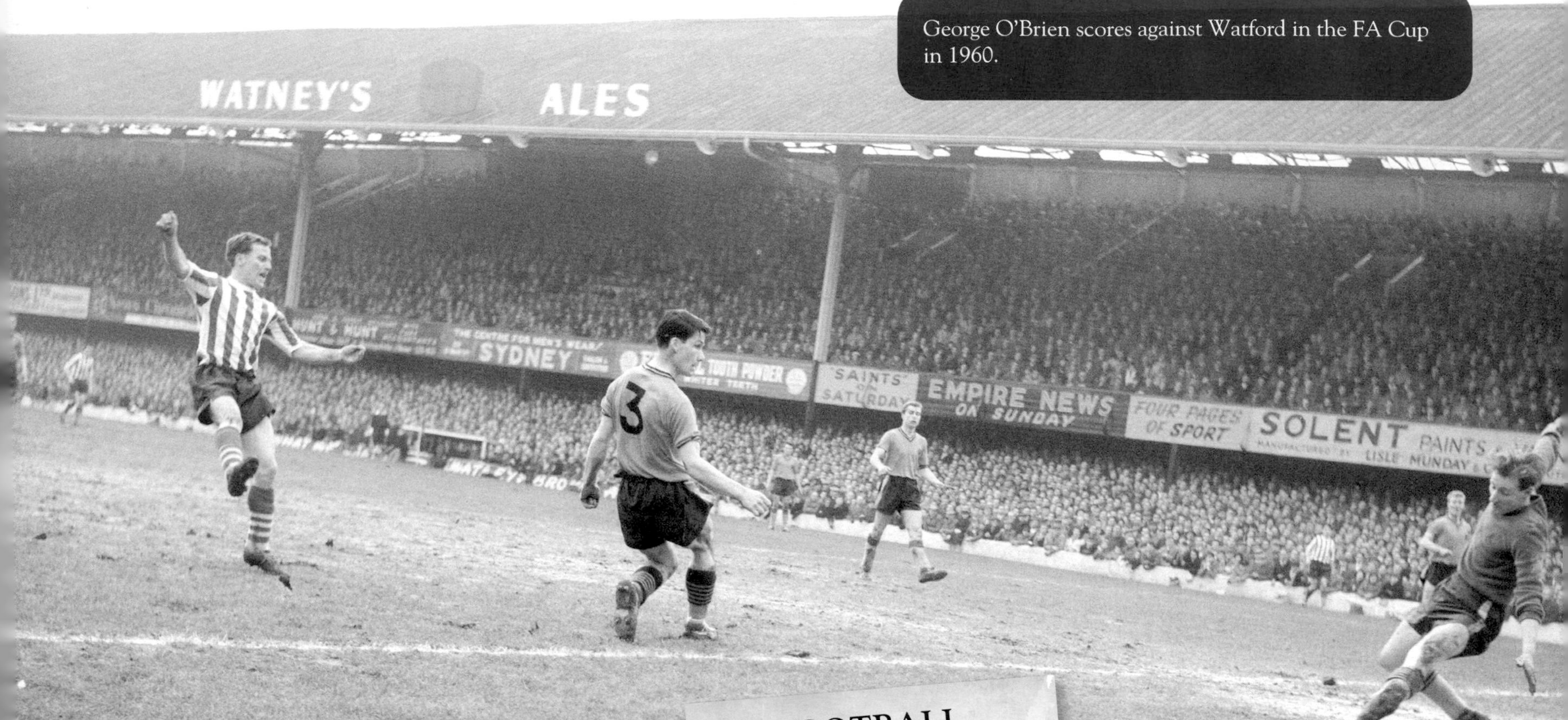

George O'Brien scores against Watford in the FA Cup in 1960.

FOOTBALL
–STATS–

George O'Brien

Name: George O'Brien

Date of Birth: 22nd November 1935

Position: Inside-forward

Playing Career: Dunfermline, Leeds, Southampton (1959–65), Leyton Orient, Aldershot

Southampton Appearances: 244

Southampton Goals: 154

Scotland Caps: 0

–LEGENDS–

George O'Brien

Having spent six years at The Dell, O'Brien became a firm favourite with the Saints faithful, and his goals-to-games ratio is second to none. He began his career with Dunfermline – his town of birth – and made over 400 league appearances for five clubs.

Robbed by the Law

Saints fans are in party mood for the FA Cup semi-final clash with Manchester United at Villa Park in April 1963. But it proves to be another false dawn as Denis Law scored the only goal of the game in front of a crowd of 68,000.

Manchester United players celebrate as the referee blows the final whistle at Villa Park.

BELOW: The *Mirror* report Southampton's meek semi-final surrender.

Days earlier, supporters had queued at The Dell for their semi-final tickets and this young fan was lucky enough to get his hands on one. Little did they know another semi-final defeat was on the cards.

Saints flop
—surrender
to a myth

BY KEN JONES

WEMBLEY is set to stage its biggest Cup Final flop, unless method is injected into the muddle that is Manchester United.

The Saints surrendered 1—0 at Villa Park, burdened by the biggest inferiority complex I've seen in a semi-final team.

They seemed mesmerised by the magic name Manchester United. And yet they had nothing to fear.

Noel Cantwell, United skipper, maintains "It is better to win in a negative fashion than to lose playing entertaining football."

Tatty

United manager Matt Busby said: "I knew that as long as we made no mistakes in defence we would go through to the final."

But as entertainment this game wouldn't have been booked for a seaside show in the Orkneys.

I looked in vain for signs of greatness from men who are supposed to be great players.

Denis Law contributed nothing except a tatty goal, and Pat Crerand spoiled a hard-working performance with a running display of bad temper.

Ted Bates, Southampton manager, told me: "We didn't touch our normal form"

Yet, Terry Paine did enough to become the game's best winger ... and he didn't have to do much to be that. George Kirby battled gamely against United's outstanding star centre half Billy Foulkes.

But, while Southampton believed in the United myth they never gave themselves a chance.

Suffering Saints ..

Southampton goalkeeper Ron Reynolds sprawls helpless in the net (left), beaten by Denis Law. This scrambled goal was the end of the Cup trail for the Second Division Saints.

45

SPORTS GOODS
ROAD ∘ PHONE 23694

Saints players training at The Dell in March 1963 before beating Huddersfield 3-1 under the ever watchful eye of Jimmy Gallagher. But away from the glamour of that thrilling FA Cup run they began the 1962–63 season in disastrous fashion and, after eight games, were bottom of the table. However, Bates was backed by the board and was able to spend £50,000 on new players. Slowly, the league form picked up and Saints lifted themselves away from the relegation zone to finish mid-table.

47

Paine's England Arrival

England boss Sir Alf Ramsey talks tactics with Terry Paine before the Southampton man won his first full England cap in June 1963. Paine made his mark on the national team in November as he scored a hat-trick at Wembley in the 8-3 win against Northern Ireland to become the first outside-right to hit three goals for England since Sir Stanley Matthews in 1937.

Paine was also prolific for Saints as he shared the goalscoring plaudits with Martin Chivers: they both finished with 21 league goals in the 1963–64 campaign. Chivers also won an England Under-23 cap.

The following season George O'Brien (32), Chivers (18) and Paine (14) terrorized the Second Division defences to help Saints top the scoring charts with 83 goals and finish fourth.

ENGLAND STORM HOME ON THE WINGS

Paine and Charlton shatter Germans

BELOW: Rampant England put eight past Northern Ireland as Jimmy Greaves and Terry Paine score seven between them.

History Boys

Terry Paine (left) wheels away in delight after scoring the goal that all but sealed Southampton's promotion to the First Division for the first time ever.

His header secured a 1-1 draw with Leyton Orient at Brisbane Road on 9th May 1966 and promotion was confirmed with a draw against champions Manchester City on the last day of the season.

BELOW: First Division here we come – the Saints' fans parade their promotion heroes across the Brisbane Road pitch.

BELOW INSET: Terry Paine grabs the headlines after his goal and, as the *Mirror* points out, only a final-day disaster can prevent Saints going up.

SOCCER

PAINE HEADS SAINTS INTO FIRST DIVISION

Only a 6-0 disaster against City can stop them now

By KEN JONES. Leyton Orient 1, Southampton 1

SOUTHAMPTON are in the First Division. Only an incredible disaster can destroy their dream now.

Thousands of their fans swelled Orient's crowd to the biggest of the season last night and poured on to the pitch after they had snatched the one point they needed with a Terry Paine goal.

They lifted Paine on to a human charge and stood chairing for their team and manager Ted Bates to come back from the dressing-room.

Saints must lose 6-0 against Manchester City on Saturday to have all last night's excitement and achievement shattered—and that surely cannot happen.

Southampton were in trouble after only eleven minutes. Caught up in the momentum of their own attack they were suddenly wide open as Orient right winger Harry Gregory gambled through to bring a fine save out of goalkeeper Campbell Forsyth.

It was a Mcoff, but the relief lasted only for one minute. A similar break caught Southampton unaware again, right half Peter Allen going through on a pass from John Smith.

This time there was no answer from Forsyth, and Southampton were a goal down and struggling.

Strangely, with only one point needed, the Saints gambled on attacking football.

Their marking was poor, their passing careless. They might have conceded another when Gregory broke clear to fire a fierce shot into the crowd for a corner.

Forsyth did well to pull it into the crowd for a

Flashes

Occasional flashes from Paine, and some parry runs from John Sydenham, suggested Southampton could change the situation.

But they had effort was header from centre forward Norman Dean after a Paine freekick.

Paine appealed in vain for a penalty when Orient scrambled the ball clear with the help of a hand.

The out-and Southampton needed to badly came in the 82nd minute.

Former Orient full back David Webb reduced an anxious goalmouth situation, then hit a hopeful ball deep into Orient territory.

A mistake by centre half Gordon Perry and 18 yard Paine to head into club into the First Division.

Torquay go top of the table

Torquay 3, Notts Co. 0

TORQUAY jumped to the top of the Fourth Division last night.

Torquay right half and skipper John Benson scored a great goal to put his side into a twelfth-minute lead.

It began with outside left Tom Barton taking the ball brilliantly upfield and beating County's defence with a magnificent cross.

Benson then had kept pace with Barton all the way, dived full length to meet the ball with his head and direct the ball the head finish could do no more than help it into the Soo.

County defended stubbornly as the Devon side hammered away for a clinching goal.

Five minutes from the end Torquay made their twelfth great opportunity goal of Tom Merritt.

SPEEDWAY

BRITISH LEAGUE:—
Swindon 51, Coventry 27. (Swindon's fourth home win.)

RESULTS AND SCORERS

FIRST DIVISION

(first names)
H.T. 7.75%
Leicester.........2
(second names)
A.T.

SECOND DIVISION

(names)
H.T. 23.056

Brentford........1
Port..............
H.T. 19,390

THIRD DIVISION

(names)
Marshall..........
Green.............
Howard............
Sanders...........
H.T. 7,197

LEICESTER COULD HAVE USED THAT BRIDGES FINISH!

By PETER INGALL   Leicester 2, West Ham 1

BARRY BRIDGES, £55,000 Chelsea and England forward, travelled to Leicester yesterday for further talks with manager Matt Gillies on his possible move to Filbert Street.

While he was still making up his mind whether to stay in First Division Soccer or accept an attractive offer from Second Division Birmingham City, Bridges stayed on to watch this entertaining game.

The Chelsea man must have been impressed with the way Leicester built up their attacks with some attractive football—but he cannot have been thinking he cut out on the field and help finish off the move.

Leicester fans are also reminded their attack could badly do with a finisher.

England angry —Wales leave him behind

By FRANK McGHEE

MIKE ENGLAND, Blackburn centre half, last night angrily attacked a decision to cut him out of the Welsh tour of South

Leyton Orient goalkeeper Vic Rouse looks as though he has lost the ball as he goes down to save from Martin Chivers

It was a fluke I think. Everybody thought I would miss it but I've got on my bike early and it's bounced over the top of them and I've headed it into the net.

Terry Paine

"

51

Martin Chivers wreaks havoc among the Leyton Orient defence, much as he did up and down the country for the whole of the 1965–66 promotion campaign.

Terry Paine may have taken the plaudits on that memorable night at Brisbane Road, but it was Chivers who was the star of the season with his 30 league goals. Amazingly, he failed to score in any of the last 13 games.

Martin Chivers had struck up a devastating partnership with George O'Brien and Terry Paine as Saints started the season in impressive form, putting six past Bury (four from O'Brien) and four past Norwich; they finally looked like they would challenge for the title.

Confirmation of their title credentials came when Chivers hit four in the 9-3 drubbing of Wolves at The Dell in September.

Paine (2), John Sydenham (2) and O'Brien completed the rout and it was just the tonic required as Saints themselves had been on the end of a 5-1 hammering four days earlier at Coventry.

Seventeen-year-old Mick Channon also made his debut during the campaign, scoring in the 2-2 draw with Bristol City on 11th April 1966.

Second Division Top Six

	P	W	D	L	F	A	Pts
Manchester City	42	22	15	5	76	44	59
Southampton	42	22	10	10	85	56	54
Coventry City	42	20	13	9	73	53	53
Huddersfield	42	19	13	10	62	36	51
Bristol City	42	17	17	8	63	48	51
Wolves	42	20	10	12	87	61	50

The fixture list for the promotion-winning campaign was a little cruel, leaving Saints with three away games to finish the season. Terry Paine was carried from the pitch by the fans after Saints' last game at The Dell on 30th April 1966. He scored the only goal of the game in a 1-0 win over Charlton in front of 22,480, to set up that historic night at Brisbane Road.

Summer 1966: Away from England's World Cup celebrations it is business as usual at club level and Ted Bates signs Welsh international Ron Davies from Norwich for a club record fee of £55,000. **February 1967:** One of the few high points of the relegation-threatened campaign is the 6-2 thrashing of West Ham at The Dell. The Hammers include World Cup winners Bobby Moore, Sir Geoff Hurst and Martin Peters. **May 1967:** Saints stay up by the skin of their teeth thanks to a 6-2 thrashing of Aston Villa – who are relegated – on the final day. Ron Davies hits four to take his season's tally to 37 and finish as the league's top scorer, ahead of Sir Geoff Hurst.

Champion of the World

The Terry Paine fairy tale rolled on as he was selected for England's 1966 World Cup squad. After firing Saints into the top flight, he played in the group stage win over Mexico.

It was Paine's only match but another Saint, Sir Alf Ramsey, masterminded England's famous 4-2 extra-time win over West Germany to lift the World Cup. A certain Alan Ball, at the tender age of 21, was one of England's driving forces and a Saints great in the making.

Terry Paine prepares for an England training session.

ABOVE: England boss Sir Alf Ramsey parades the Jules Rimet trophy before a banquet at the Royal Garden Hotel in London. Terry Paine can't help but give it an admiring glance along with Ron Springett (far left) and George Cohen (middle).

LEFT: Terry Paine eats breakfast with John Connelly, Ian Callaghan, Jimmy Greaves, Roger Hunt and Jimmy Armfield at the England team hotel during the 1966 World Cup.

ABOVE: Southampton goalkeeper Campbell Forsyth claims this cross off the head of Derek Dougan. Wolves won the game 2-0 at Molineux as Saints again struggled to adapt in the top flight. But the ever reliable Ron Davies stamped his authority on the 1967–68 league campaign as he hit four goals in Southampton's 6-2 hammering of Chelsea at Stamford Bridge in September.

He finished as joint top scorer, alongside the great George Best, with 28.

Saints and Newcastle players go toe-to-toe on the opening day of the 1967–68 season in front of a packed St James' Park. The Magpies won the game 3-0.

Get Your Bananas...

LEFT: The glamour of top-flight football. Terry Paine gets down to the business of sorting his fruit and veg at the greengrocer's store he opened on the outskirts of Southampton. Players in the late 1960s could make a decent living from the game but nothing like that which even the average player gets today – let alone what an England international of Paine's class would earn.

Chivers Quits The Dell

Unsettled Martin Chivers was sold to Spurs for £125,000 in January 1968, making him the country's most expensive footballer. Frank Saul, pictured here with Chivers at The Dell, came the other way as part of the deal and, with Mick Channon emerging as a great talent, it proved to be an inspired piece of business by Ted Bates.

BELOW: Martin Chivers hands in a transfer request – but Saints vow to try and keep their man.

ABOVE & BELOW: Tottenham-bound Martin Chivers helps Frank Saul settle into his new surroundings at The Dell.

DAILY MIRROR, Monday, December 18, 1967   PAGE 19

£120,000 CHIVERS TRAIL

But Southampton will try to hold on to their unhappy striker

By HARRY MILLER

MARTIN CHIVERS, Southampton striker, wrote a transfer request yesterday that could make him a £120,000-plus target for at least six top clubs.

Arsenal, Spurs and Sunderland are all potential bidders. Manchester United, Nottingham Forest and Wolves will all be interested.

And many managers will watch Chivers in Wednesday's Under-23 international between England and Italy at Nottingham—just twenty-four hours before the Southampton directors meet to consider his request.

I expect them to make every effort to keep their unhappy star.

Manager Ted Bates has succeeded before in persuading players like Terry Paine, Ron Davies and David Webb to stay at The Dell.

But the sort of fee 22-year-old Chivers would command must be tempting.

Southampton have spent around £200,000 in the past two years to establish themselves in the First Division. They haven't been sellers.

Policy

Last night Bates told me : "We got in the First Division by holding on to our players. We want to stay there with the same policy.

"I know it can be disturbing for a boy in Martin's class when he keeps reading about £100,000 deals going on in the game.

"The way it's going, £130,000 for a player is just around the corner. I certainly can't say what I think Martin is worth. I don't value players who are not for sale."

I understand Chivers feels that Southampton are limited in what they can achieve by the size of their ground and gate potential.

Manchester United legend George Best weaves his way through the Southampton defence to score in October 1968. After two years of struggling following promotion, Saints at last began to find their feet in the top flight, as demonstrated by this 2-1 win at Old Trafford. Ron Davies was again instrumental with 20 goals, and the seventh-place finish in the 1968–69 campaign was the Saints' highest ever.

Southampton defenders crowd out Everton winger Jimmy Husband in December 1968, with Joe Royle (No. 9) ready to pounce.

Ron Top of the World

Ron Davies scored all four goals in Southampton's stunning 4-1 win over a Manchester United side including George Best, Denis Law and Sir Bobby Charlton at Old Trafford on 16th August 1969.

Davies said: "The biggest thrill of my life was going to Old Trafford and scoring four goals. Busby said to me, 'Ron, I've been after you for years. They won't let you go.'

"I would have gone in a heartbeat and relished the opportunity of winning a few more medals. Maybe I wouldn't have done so well because I think Painie was a better player then Willie Morgan and on the left-hand side, I had Sydenham."

> "
> He looked like the greatest centre-forward in the world against us.
>
> Sir Matt Busby
> "

BELOW: Manchester United boss Sir Matt Busby praises Ron Davies in the *Mirror* after he single-handedly demolished the Red Devils.

Ron Davies is the greatest No 9 in the world

By HARRY MILLER

THAT'S MATT'S VERDICT AND HERE IS SOME OF THE PROOF

Terry Paine in full flight at Old Trafford. Along with John Sydenham, Paine provided ammunition for the prolific Ron Davies during his time at The Dell.

Southampton's return to Manchester later that season was not so triumphant. Mick Channon is robbed of the ball by City's Mike Doyle in the 1-0 defeat at Maine Road. Despite Ron Davies' heroics at Old Trafford, it was Channon who topped the scoring charts for Saints with 15 goals as they just stayed up.

RIGHT: Captain Terry Paine leads Southampton out against Crystal Palace at Selhurst Park in October 1970.

> "He's a great player. He's not the biggest centre-forward but he'd just hang in the air. Unbelievable."
>
> Peter Osgood

> "When Ron doesn't score he's miserable, but he always works to put it right. Above all he plays for the team, and it's his value to the team that's important."
>
> Ted Bates

Ron Davies relaxes at home with his family during Christmas 1969.

–LEGENDS–

Ron Davies

Ted Bates signed Ron Davies for a club record £55,000 from Norwich after Southampton's promotion to the top flight in 1966. Already an established Welsh international, Davies scored 12 goals in 10 consecutive league games and ended the season as the division's top scorer with 37 goals in 41 games.

He was joint top marksman the following season –1967–68 – with George Best. But a series of injuries reduced his effectiveness and, by 1973, Davies was unable to hold down a regular place in the first team.

He joined Portsmouth in April 1973, and scored 18 goals in 59 games. Manchester United, who had coveted Davies for most of his career, eventually got their man in November 1974, but his playing opportunities were limited.

FOOTBALL –STATS–

Ron Davies

Name: Ron Davies

Date of Birth: 25th May 1942

Position: Forward

Playing Career: Chester, Luton, Norwich, Southampton (1966–73), Portsmouth, Man United

Southampton Appearances: 240

Southampton Goals: 134

Wales Caps: 29

Ron Davies was brilliant in the air but Leeds goalkeeper Gary Sprake gets the better of him here.

Euro Stars

Southampton's better showing in the league propelled them into the European positions – and new territory.

They made their debut in the Inter-Cities Fairs Cup in 1969–70 thanks to the one team per city rule that unfairly penalized the London clubs.

Saints made a good account of themselves, beating Rosenborg and Vitória SC of Portugal before Newcastle halted their progress on the away goals rule in the third round.

But it was the start of some great European nights at The Dell throughout the 1970s and early 1980s.

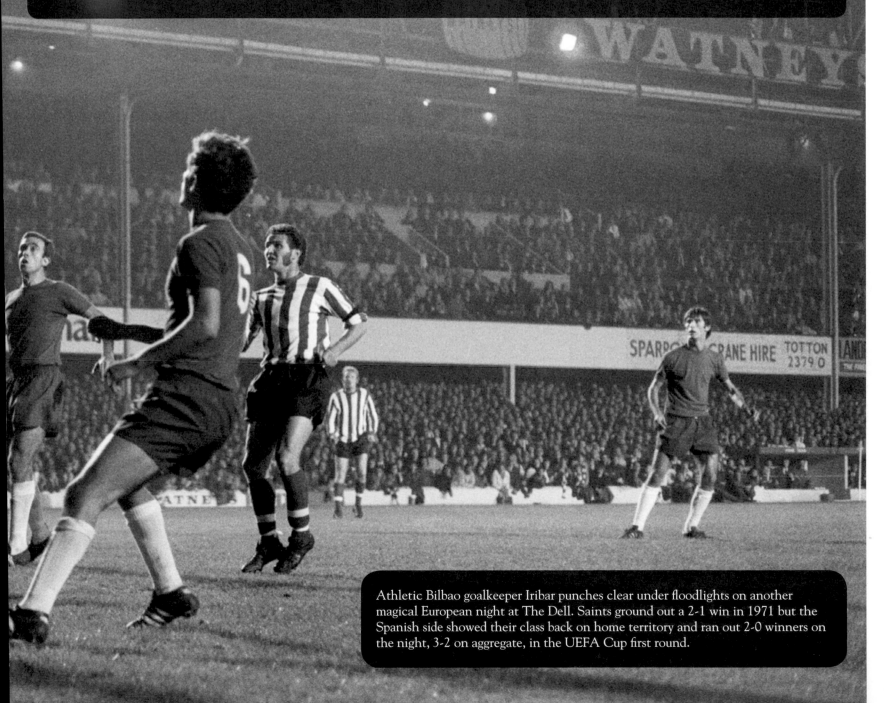

Athletic Bilbao goalkeeper Iribar punches clear under floodlights on another magical European night at The Dell. Saints ground out a 2-1 win in 1971 but the Spanish side showed their class back on home territory and ran out 2-0 winners on the night, 3-2 on aggregate, in the UEFA Cup first round.

Channon on the Rise

Mick Channon lifts the ball over Spurs keeper Pat Jennings to score one of his two goals in the 3-1 win at White Hart Lane. Channon had become a key figure for Southampton and his 18 goals in the 1970–71 campaign helped Saints to seventh place and UEFA Cup qualification.

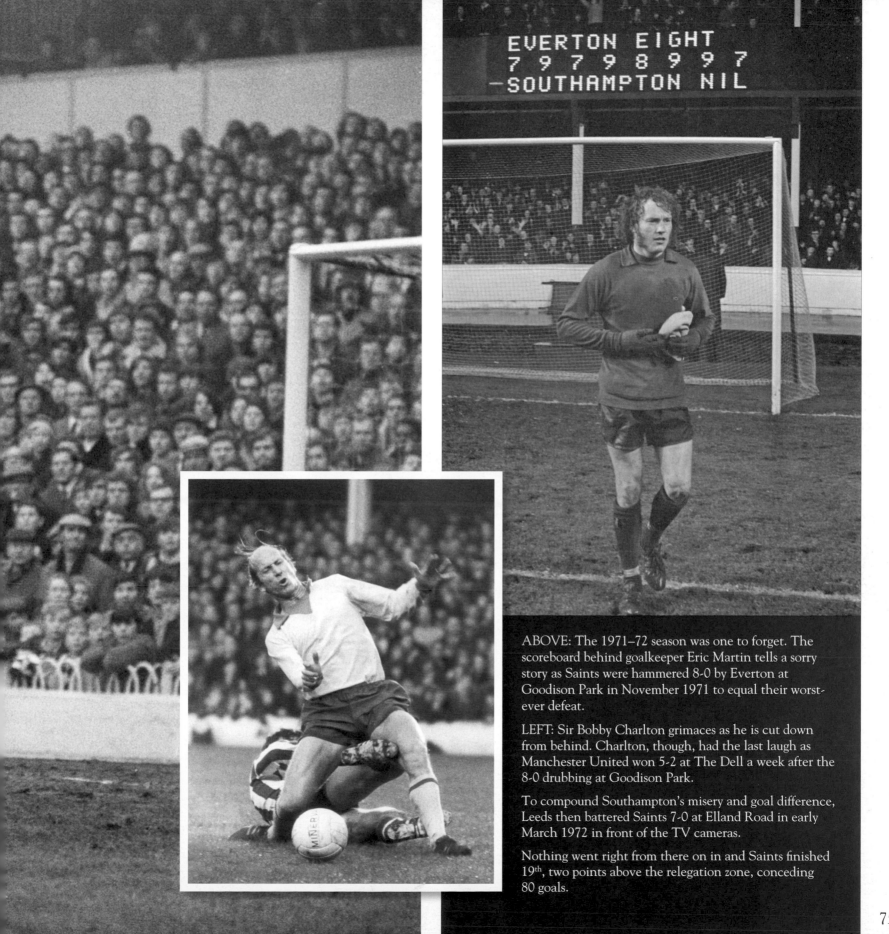

EVERTON EIGHT
7 9 7 9 8 9 9 7
—SOUTHAMPTON NIL

ABOVE: The 1971–72 season was one to forget. The scoreboard behind goalkeeper Eric Martin tells a sorry story as Saints were hammered 8-0 by Everton at Goodison Park in November 1971 to equal their worst-ever defeat.

LEFT: Sir Bobby Charlton grimaces as he is cut down from behind. Charlton, though, had the last laugh as Manchester United won 5-2 at The Dell a week after the 8-0 drubbing at Goodison Park.

To compound Southampton's misery and goal difference, Leeds then battered Saints 7-0 at Elland Road in early March 1972 in front of the TV cameras.

Nothing went right from there on in and Saints finished 19th, two points above the relegation zone, conceding 80 goals.

David Walker and John McGrath (right) arrive at the Great Western Hotel, Paddington, London, to attend a disciplinary hearing in January 1972.

End of an Era

The 1972–73 campaign proved to be the end of an era at The Dell. Fortunes on the field improved and Saints steered clear of a relegation fight but it was Ted Bates' last season in charge. The irrepressible Ron Davies requested a move as injuries began to take a toll.

On a positive note, Mick Channon continued to flourish and was rewarded with his first England cap in October 1972 in the 1-1 draw with Yugoslavia at Wembley.

And Jim Steele, an £80,000 club record signing from Dundee, shored up a leaky defence that had struggled to cope with top-flight strikers in previous seasons.

LEFT: Ron Davies warms up before the clash with Wolves at The Dell in 1972 – but it was to be his last season in a Saints shirt before signing for Portsmouth in April 1973.

BELOW: *Mirror* man Frank McGhee's match report gives Mick Channon the thumbs up on his England debut. The Southampton man's performance was full of "stealth and power".

PAGE 30 DAILY MIRROR, Thursday, October 12, 1972

BIG NIGHT AT WEMBLEY

ENGLAND DEFY

FLYING GOALKEEPER . . . Maric catapults through the air as he stops an England shot in the drawn international at Wembley last night.

England 1, Yugoslavia 1
(At Wembley. H-T.: 1—0. Att.: 50,000)

YUGOSLAVIA have something England lack—a genuine 24 carat world-class winger of pace, grace, skill and subtlety.

That is why all the pleasure and pride in what was essentially an impressive performance by a depleted England side, at Wembley last night, has to be tempered with caution, soured slightly by lingering doubts.

A fifteen-minute spell of dazzling football by outside left Dragan Dzajic — the surname rhymes with "magic" and that is no coincidence — distorts the over-all image and memory of the match.

In the last quarter-of-an-hour, England could have had this draw taken away from them and reshaped into a defeat that, over the whole match, would have been a terrible injustice.

In the 78th minute Dzajic sliced across one of those deadly swerving shots that are his speciality, watched the ball bounce out of goalkeeper Peter Shilton's arms—then held his head as Petkovic, from five yards, steered it wide.

Lunging

In the 85th minute, Dzajic did not so much beat Mick Mills as ignore him, brushing past him and providing a cross that Bajevic deflected six inches too far to the right — into the side-netting.

In the 88th minute, with the England defence lunging, plunging, lost and missing, he checked, put his toe under the ball, and lobbed it in a dipping arc against the bar.

Happily, it could not entirely obscure the most important point of the match—the emergence of two new strikers for England.

The most pleasant task

for any sportswriter is to record the successful arrival on the international scene of a new boy—and Southampton's Mick Channon provided the opportunity with a performance of stealth and power.

He was only a shade behind a man with just one more cap—Everton's Joe Royle, all hustle, muscle and drive.

Unfortunately, both did so much work that they tired. But then the knowledge and ability to pace a match at top-level is something they can still learn.

I cannot feel as happy about the new right back, Mick Mills—but he, of course, had the unenviable task of marking Dzajic.

In fact I cannot understand why, with three right-footed midfield players, Sir Alf Ramsey didn't use the most tigerish of them, Peter Storey, on the right of the field in support.

Nor can I understand why, when Colin Bell

THE VOICE OF SPORT..

FRANK McGHEE

ALWAYS WHERE THE ACTION IS

visibly tired towards the end, Howard Kendall was not substituted.

Still, that is carping criticism, perhaps. Apart from the Dzajic magic—with no apologies for either the pun or the poetry—the outstanding memory of the match was the goal England scored in the 40th minute.

The great goals are made up of many things —and this had most of them.

Superb

It contained the superb accuracy of the two passes that set it up, from Rodney Marsh out of defence to Bell, and from Bell into the penalty-area.

It contained the coolness of Channon, who pulled it back with the sole of his boot out of goalkeeper Maric's despairing grab and then raced away from goal to create the space to turn and look.

It contained the un-

GROUNDED . . . England's Peter Shilton is beaten by Vladic in a flat-out finish after Bajevic had headed the ball down from a Krivokuva cross.   *Picture: PETER STONE*

77

1973-1985

"I just like to think I built on Ted's groundwork. The foundations were right. Ted as a bloke is a one-off. The word legend is misused but, in Ted's case, it's an apt word. Ted deserves everything, and more, of the work he did in the early days."

Lawrie McMenemy

Lawrie McMenemy took over from Ted Bates as manager in July 1973, but his tenure got off to the worst possible start as Saints were relegated from the top flight.

They had won just three of their last 15 games, and had experienced a terrible collapse over the Easter period. Despite beating Everton 3-0 on the last day at Goodison Park, it was clear the footballing gods were not smiling on McMenemy as it was the first season the three-down rule applied, meaning Saints slipped out of the top flight by one point, along with Manchester United and Norwich.

Hugh Fisher presents Leeds hardman Norman Hunter with a bunch of flowers before kick-off in January 1974. It didn't do Saints much good as they lost 2-1 at Elland Road.

Lawrie McMenemy and Ted Bates arrive at Highbury for a league managers' meeting in November 1973. With the Southampton men is newly appointed Norwich City boss John Bond.

LEFT: Alan Hudson keeps a close eye on Saints' new boy Peter Osgood during Stoke's 4-1 win in March 1974. It was one of Osgood's first matches after signing for a club record fee of £235,000.

OSSIE ON MOVE AT £285,000 'SINNER' TURNS SAINT

He makes a deadly link with Channon

By NIGEL CLARKE

REBEL HUTCH

Terry Paine MBE

This brilliant winger was made captain in August 1961 and his and the club's fortunes prospered. He was an ever-present player for a record seven seasons, and his 713 league appearances are a club record. Not content with being one of the greatest footballers of his era, Terry Paine was also an astute businessman. He opened a greengrocer's store on the outskirts of the city and was a Conservative councillor for Bargate on Southampton Borough Council for three years. Now living in South Africa, he remains a Saints legend through and through.

FOOTBALL —STATS—

Terry Paine MBE

Name: Terry Paine

Date of Birth: 23rd March 1939

Position: Forward

Playing Career: Southampton (1956–74), Hereford

Southampton Appearances: 713

Southampton Goals: 160

Managerial Career: Cheltenham Town

England Caps: 19

LEFT: Councillor Terry Paine leaves Southampton Town Hall in 1969, passing a saluting sergeant-at-arms, Mr Charles Watson.

RIGHT: Terry Paine, a substitute in the famous 4-2 win over West Germany, collects his World Cup-winning medal from Prime Minister Gordon Brown in 2009.

Terry Paine turns out in the World Cup Commemoration and Royal Jubilee five-a-side at Wembley in 1977. Alongside him are Jimmy Greaves, Sir Geoff Hurst, Ron Springett, Sir Alf Ramsey, Nobby Stiles, Harold Shepperton and Bobby Moore.

1974: Lawrie McMenemy begins the unenviable task of rebuilding after relegation. **September 1974:** Beat Scottish giants Rangers 3-1 at Ibrox in the Texaco Anglo-Scottish Cup. McMenemy, under fire from restless fans, said: "Not many teams win at Ibrox, let alone so convincingly. Our front-runners revelled in the open spaces." **October 1974:** Beat Rangers 2-0 at The Dell in the second leg. **November 1974:** Oldham are no match and go down 5-2 on aggregate in the Texaco Anglo-Scottish Cup semi-final. **December 1974:** Mick Channon scores the only goal as they beat Newcastle 1-0 in the first leg of the Texaco Anglo-Scottish Cup final at The Dell. The return at St James' Park goes to extra-time but Newcastle win 3-0 on the night. **February 1975:** Lawrie McMenemy signs experienced midfielder Jim McCalliog from Manchester United for £45,000. **April 1975:** Despite Mick Channon's 20 goals, Saints' league form is erratic and they finish in a disappointing mid-table position.

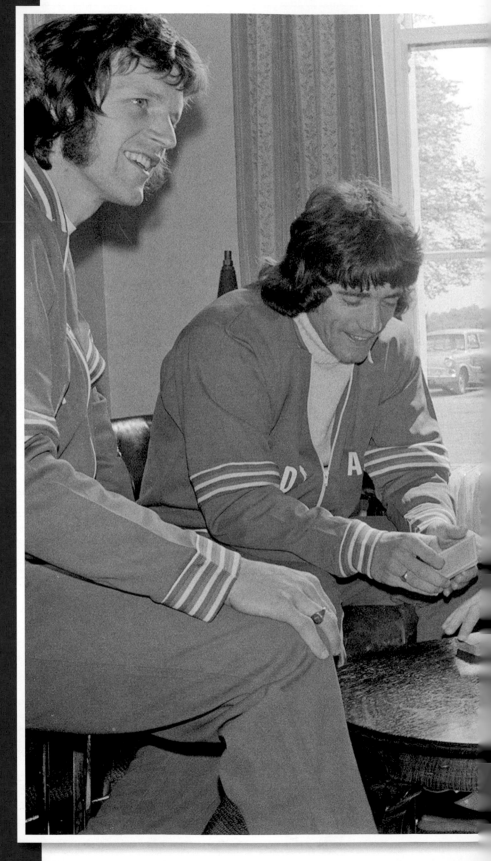

LEFT: Mick Channon had become an England regular by 1975 and is here deep in conversation with David Johnson while Kevin Keegan and Alan Ball play cards at the table.

BELOW: Mick Channon is shown a clean set of heels by England manager Don Revie during a training session in 1976.

LEFT: There have been plenty of colourful fans at The Dell down the years, and none more so than this immaculately dressed gentleman in 1975.

Ted MacDougall proved himself to be a hotshot on the pitch for Southampton but here he gets hold of something a little more powerful than his left foot with the Royal Anglian Regiment on Salisbury Plain.

ABOVE & BELOW: Peter Rodrigues and Mick Channon set their sights on the target and prepare to fire.

Proof, if it were ever needed, that football really was a different game back in the 1970s as the ever-meticulous Lawrie McMenemy prepares his players for their clash with Chelsea. There's no fancy technology here, just a good old-fashioned board perched on a stool and some discs representing player movements.

Cup Kings

Bobby Stokes, in the bath at Wembley with Peter Osgood, kisses the FA Cup after his goal sealed a brilliant victory over Manchester United.

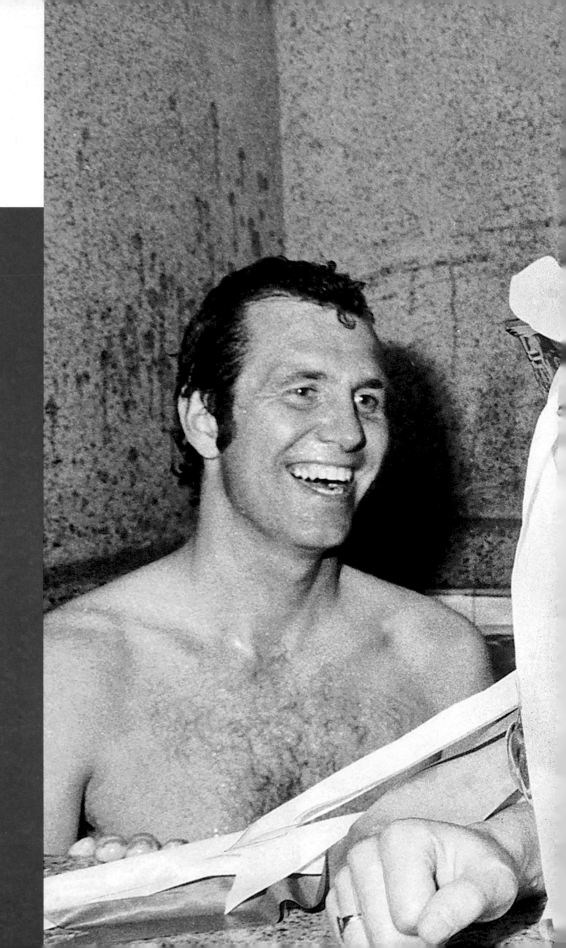

> "It was the highlight of my career. I dined out on it more times than I can remember. I did not play for Saints as long as I would have liked, but I played in the one that mattered.
>
> Bobby Stokes on his Wembley winner

Mick Channon scores the first of his hat-trick in the FA Cup fifth-round replay against West Brom at The Dell.

Mick Channon jumps on Paul Gilchrist's back after Gilchrist's stunning overhead kick put Saints two-up against West Brom.

3rd January 1976: Third round

Southampton 1   **Aston Villa 1**
(Fisher 89)   (Gray 64)
Attendance: 24,138

Hugh Fisher, who scored just 11 goals in 356 competitive appearances for the club, hits a last-minute equalizer at The Dell.

Mick Channon said: "It's strange, but things happened in the cup run which were almost weird. Afterwards, I said, 'Well, Hughie's just scored, we'll win the FA Cup now.' He never scores."

7th January 1976: Third-round replay

Aston Villa 1   **Southampton 2 (AET)**
(Graydon 39)   (McCalliog 31, 103)
Attendance: 44,623

Jim McCalliog headed home Mick Channon's cross to give Saints the lead but Ray Graydon sent the tie to extra-time. McCalliog settled it with a deflected shot from David Peach's corner.

Aston Villa defender Chris Nicholl – who would later become a Saints player and then manager – said: "We made the mistake of thinking we had done the hard work and would have no trouble back at our place."

24th January 1976: Fourth round

Southampton 3   **Blackpool 1**
(Channon 5, 67   (Hatton 89)
Stokes 56)
Attendance: 21,553

Mick Channon's early goal settled the nerves and Saints never looked back. Bobby Stokes doubled the lead before Channon put the tie beyond doubt. Goalkeeper Ian Turner said: "You always fancy yourself at home. We had a great home record that season and we only missed out on promotion because of our away form."

14th February 1976: Fifth round

West Brom 1
(Brown 58)
Attendance: 36,634

Southampton 1
(Stokes 75)

Mick Channon, Bobby Stokes and Nick Holmes are laid low with a stomach bug.

Stokes, who cancelled out Tony Brown's opener, was particularly ill on the morning of the match.

"A few of the guys were on their knees," recalls Fisher. "We had a small squad and there was only one substitute allowed so we were up against it."

17th February 1976: Fifth-round replay

Southampton 4
(Channon 1, 30, pen 74
Gilchrist 17)
Attendance: 27,614

West Brom 0

Mick Channon stole the headlines with a hat-trick – but Paul Gilchrist scored with a stunning overhead kick.

Gilchrist, who replaced the suspended Peter Osgood, said: "They were a very good side and hard to beat but it was one of those incredible nights at The Dell. My goal was one I do remember."

6th March 1976: Sixth round

Bradford 0

Attendance: 14,195

Southampton 1
(McCalliog 41)

With Saints safely into the sixth round, they faced an anxious wait for the outcome of the Norwich–Bradford tie, which had twice been postponed due to a flu epidemic in the Bantams' camp.

Everyone assumed First Division Norwich would prevail but the Fourth Division side sprung a shock – much to the delight of the Southampton camp.

There was, of course, still the small matter of prevailing at Valley Parade but Jim McCalliog combined with Peter Osgood's flicked up free-kick to score the winner.

McCalliog said: "We had done it a few times in training. I told Ossie to flick it up and I hit it as sweet as a nut. As soon as I hit it, I knew it was in."

Lawrie McMenemy swings a Saints shirt through the air the morning after their 4-0 replay win over West Brom at The Dell.

Saints players gather around the wireless as the semi-final draw is made. They can't hide their delight as they are paired with Third Division Crystal Palace, avoiding First Division giants Manchester United and Derby.

"
It's the first time a Cup Final will be played at Hillsborough. The other semi-final is a bit of a joke.

Tommy Docherty
"

Sun, Sea and a Cup Semi-final

Saints stars look relaxed on the beach at the picturesque Frinton-on-Sea. Boss Lawrie McMenemy took the squad away for a little R&R before the FA Cup semi-final with Crystal Palace.

But the sea air did not agree with Peter Rodrigues, Jim Steele and Jim McCalliog, who broke a curfew to go in search of late-night refreshment.

Rodrigues said: "We weren't drunk or anything but we missed the curfew. We thought we'd got away with it but Lawrie named the three of us in front of everyone the next morning and said, 'If we lose on Saturday then I'm blaming the three of you.' My head just dropped – and so did the other two."

ABOVE: I do like to be beside the seaside. Peter Rodrigues and Peter Osgood enjoy the views from the beach at Frinton-on-Sea.

Lawrie McMenemy plots Crystal Palace's cup downfall while sitting in a wheelbarrow driven by Jim Steele along the beach.

There are no outside pressures, only the players eating and sleeping football together.

Lawrie McMenemy on Saints' break to Frinton-on-Sea

Mick Channon takes a dip in the sea.

LEFT & RIGHT:
Peter Osgood and
Mick Channon mess
around on the beach.

We're All Going to Wembley

3rd April 1976: Semi-final (Stamford Bridge)

Crystal Palace 0   **Southampton 2**
.   (Gilchrist 74,
                                    Peach pen 79)

Attendance: 52,810

After years of semi-final heartbreak, Saints finally lay the ghosts to rest and reach the FA Cup final.

Paul Gilchrist put Saints in the driving seat after 74 minutes and, five minutes later, David Peach scored from the penalty spot to secure their place at Wembley.

Peach said: "Normally I pick a side and go with it but this time I just smashed it and their keeper went the wrong way. We knew we were there."

RIGHT: Paul Gilchrist is mobbed after he scores the opening goal after 74 minutes – and Saints fans go wild on the Stamford Bridge terraces in the background.

BELOW: Jim McCalliog is held back by the referee Pat Partridge as tempers fray at Stamford Bridge.

ABOVE: David Peach's (out of shot) penalty hits the back of the net and Saints know they are in the final.

BELOW: Jim Steele counters the aerial threat of Crystal Palace with a towering header as Peter Osgood looks on.

Jim McCalliog and Peter Osgood lead the celebrations in the bath.

Lawrie McMenemy does his bit for the press and leaves Stamford Bridge in a rather fetching bowler hat.

Much of the media attention had focused on Third Division Crystal Palace thanks to their colourful boss Malcolm Allison.

The fedora-wearing Palace boss (pictured left on the pitch before kick-off) courted publicity throughout their incredible cup run, and Mel Blyth struck up a bet with Allison on the pitch before the game.

Allison put three fingers up to the Crystal Palace fans, indicating that would be the winning margin and, quick as a flash, Blyth responded: "There's no way you are going to beat us today and we had a bet. I bet him his fedora against £50."

BELOW: Palace boss Malcolm Allison's bold prediction, reported on the back of the *Mirror* on the morning of the match, was way off the mark.

LEFT: Semi-final goal heroes David Peach (left) and Paul Gilchrist enjoy their moment back on the pitch in the Stamford Bridge goal long after the fans have left the ground – and seal the win with a kiss in the dressing room (below).

> "My arse was twitching. Normally I am fine with a penalty but I knew if I scored I was going to Wembley."
>
> David Peach

Spellbinding

Hypnotist Romark celebrates Southampton's FA Cup semi-final win over Crystal Palace, complete with halo. He claimed it was his curse that knocked Malcolm Allison's team out of the competition. Romark, former TV and stage illusionist Ronald Markham, claimed to have put a spell on Big Mal and Palace after Allison failed to keep an appointment at his Harley Street offices.

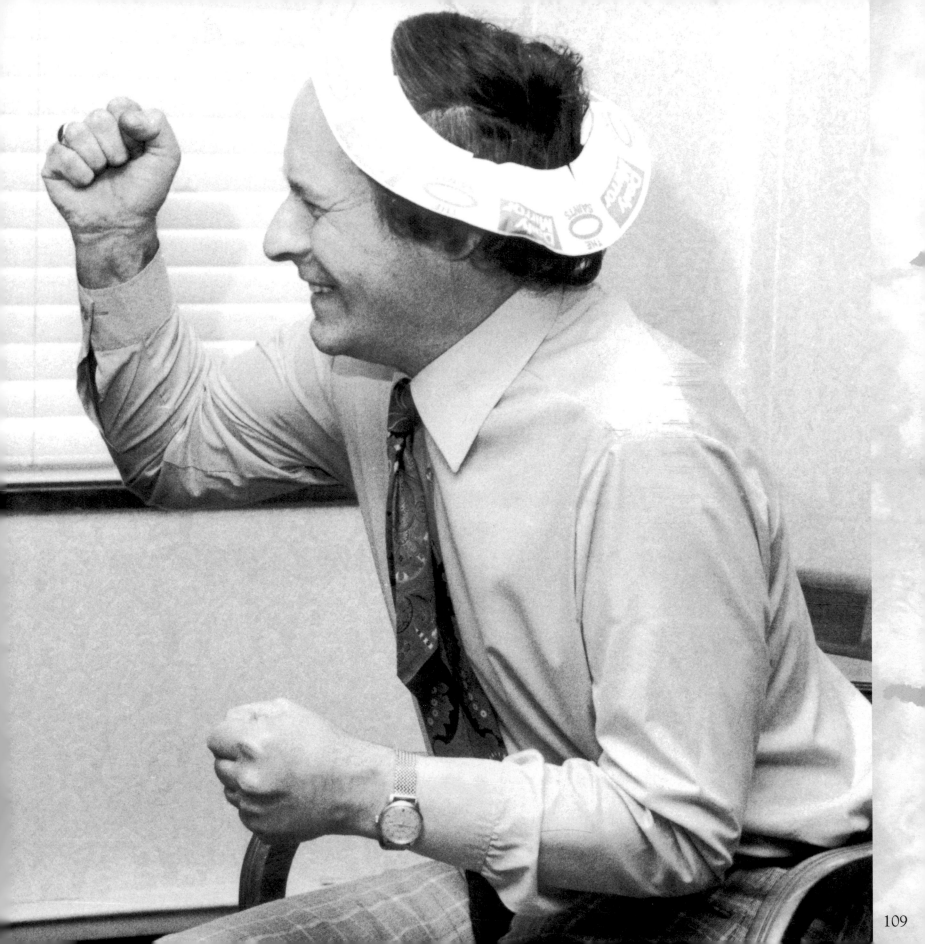

–LEGENDS–

Mick Channon

Mick Channon made 510 appearances and scored 185 goals, and tops the club's all-time scorers list. He was part of the cup-winning team of 1976, but left soon after for Manchester City in a £300,000 deal. However, he struggled to settle there, scoring just 12 goals in his first season and 11 in his second. But it was to Southampton's benefit as Channon returned to The Dell in September 1979. He is now a hugely successful racehorse trainer.

FOOTBALL –STATS–

Mick Channon

Name: Mick Channon

Date of Birth: 28th November 1948

Position: Forward

Playing Career: Southampton (1965–77), Man City, Southampton (1979–82), Newcastle, Bristol Rovers, Norwich, Portsmouth, Finn Harps

Southampton Appearances: 510

Southampton Goals: 185

England Caps: 46

> " The two loves of my life have been football and horses. Horses were my hobby but have become my life and I certainly don't regret a thing. "
>
> Mick Channon

Mick Channon at home with his family – and dogs – in March 1977.

Golden Ticket

The clamour for cup final tickets reached fever pitch as Saints fans arrived from all parts of the world and The Dell ticket office was inundated. These three lucky ladies show off the hottest tickets in town.

LEFT: Nothing was going to stop these Saints fans from getting their hands on a ticket. The queue snaked down The Dell car park and into Milton Road as fans settled in for a long wait.

BELOW: Club secretary Keith Honey holds up the sign all Saints fans dreaded seeing. FA Cup final tickets are sold out.

113

Cut Above

ABOVE: New haircuts and suit fittings have become a tradition down the years in the build-up to the FA Cup final. Jim McCalliog, Jim Steele and Peter Osgood take some time out for a short back and sides at Mr Wolf's hairdressing salon.

LEFT: Mirror, mirror on the wall, who's the hairiest of them all. Looks like you, Nick, despite a haircut and beard trim!

Mick Channon perches on top of a six-a-side goal, looking relaxed, during one of Southampton's final training sessions before the cup final.

117

Lawrie McMenemy tries on an Arab headdress sent to him for good luck by a Saint's fan in Abu Dhabi. It seemed to do the trick as he swapped this pot for another one with slightly more importance days later.

Saints hardman Jim Steele finds time to relax at The Dell – but he incurred the wrath of boss Lawrie McMenemy leading up to the final.

Along with Jim McCalliog and Peter Osgood they broke a curfew and were fined and dropped for the 1-0 win over Portsmouth at Fratton Park, where Mick Channon's goal all but relegated Pompey.

Steele, though, blamed McMenemy, albeit tongue-in-cheek, for letting them make their own way to the hotel on Hayling Island.

"He used to do it all the time. We'd go up to the sports centre and train and then he'd tell us to make our own way back. One day Ossie and I got the bus back and started waving at the lads down Hill Lane. He fined us £40 for that!" he said.

Sinning Saints must sweat it out

By JACK STEGGLES

THE three sinning Saints — Peter Osgood, Jim Steele and Jim McCalliog — may not play against Manchester United in the FA Cup Final on May 1.

All three were heavily fined and disciplined for a late-night spree before Tuesday's match at Portsmouth.

They were dropped from that game and ordered to leave the team's Hayling Island headquarters.

And now manager Lawrie McMenemy must decide whether to forgive and try to forget in the run-up to Wembley.

Waiting

He said last night: "The three players trained this morning and are available for Saturday's home match against Blackpool.

"I'll choose the team I feel is best equipped to get a good result from that game—but I have no intention of announcing it yet."

McMenemy still feels that promotion is a possibility if Southampton win all their six remaining Second Division matches.

He may bring back his wayward stars, but he could stick to the team who beat Pompey 1—0, giving Saints only their third away win of the season.

WAGs' Style 1976

Saints players' wives and girlfriends added a little glamour and style to the occasion. They stayed in the Royal Garden Hotel in Kensington the night before the final.

ABOVE: Saints stars Jim McCalliog, Mick Channon, Peter Rodrigues and Peter Osgood flex their muscles as they relax the day before the final.

BELOW: The cup gods seemed to be smiling on Southampton as the ladies showed the men how it's done. They beat QPR 2-1 after extra-time to win the Mitre Cup – the equivalent of the FA Cup – days before the Wembley showpiece.

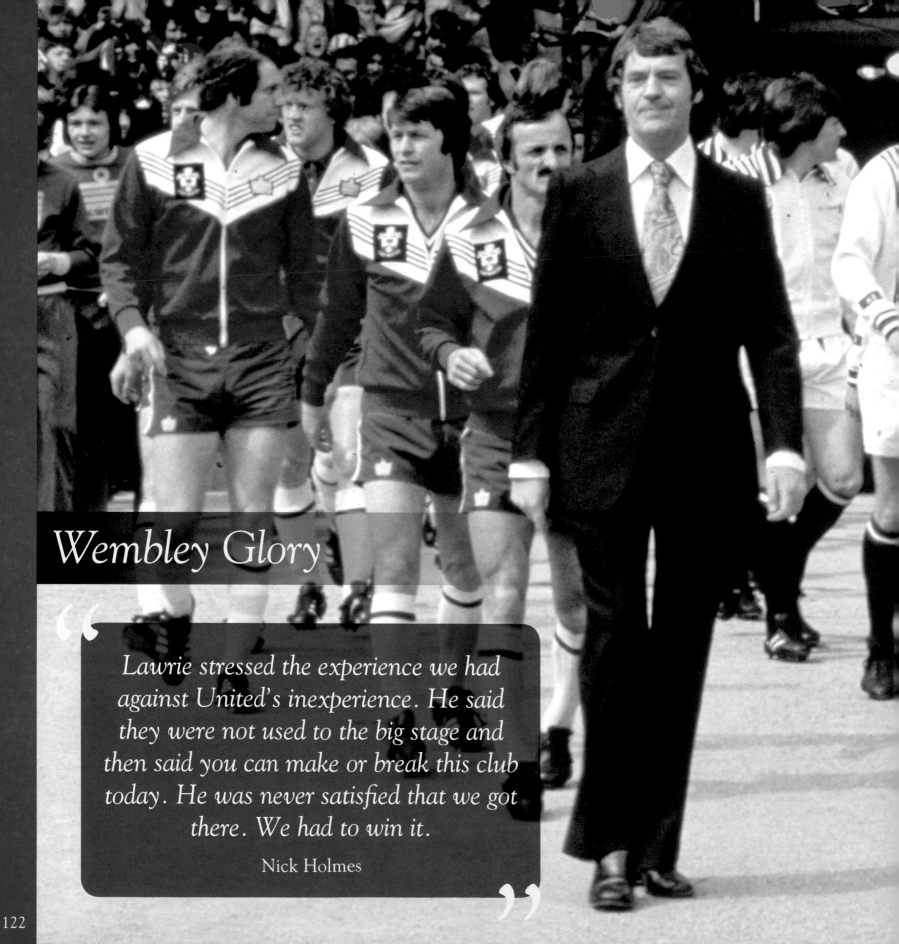

Wembley Glory

> *Lawrie stressed the experience we had against United's inexperience. He said they were not used to the big stage and then said you can make or break this club today. He was never satisfied that we got there. We had to win it.*
>
> Nick Holmes

"

A lot of our players were familiar with Wembley. The last hour before the game was the worst. You just want to bring it on. I remember how hot it was as we came up the tunnel. We were nervous, of course, and we were sweating. There were 100,000 people.

Mick Channon

"

BELOW & INSET: Ian Turner pulled off a string of fine saves – the best from Gordon Hill in the first half – as Manchester United threatened to overrun Southampton.

"

Ian had the game of his life. In the opening 20 minutes we were under siege but he was stopping everything. Half of it was with his knee, with his ankle or his elbow but he was brave as a bull and we weathered the storm.

Lawrie McMenemy

"

ABOVE: Sammy McIlroy hits the bar for United as Peter Rodrigues and Mel Blyth look on.

ABOVE: Nick Holmes and Peter Osgood bring Sammy McIlroy's probing run to an end.

Paul Gilchrist gives no quarter as he goes flying into a tackle.

Lawrie McMenemy leads the celebrations on the Southampton bench after Bobby Stokes' goal. But for Manchester United boss Tommy Docherty the pain was all too real.

We weren't overconfident but we were very confident we would win. But, on the day, we only played as well as we were allowed to. A few hours after the final I called Lawrie to congratulate him. I was disappointed but delighted for Southampton. I always had a great affection for the club.

Tommy Docherty

ABOVE: Bobby Stokes, with his arms aloft, celebrates probably the most famous goal in Southampton's history.

LEFT: Lawrie McMenemy shakes hands with match-winner Bobby Stokes on the pitch. Next to him, Ian Turner and Peter Rodrigues embrace with the FA Cup.

Party Time

Peter Rodrigues is hoisted into the air with the FA Cup as Southampton start the celebrations, following their 1-0 victory.

ABOVE & RIGHT: Southampton players begin the celebrations on the
Wembley pitch after their stunning 1-0 win over Manchester United.

Bobby Dazzler

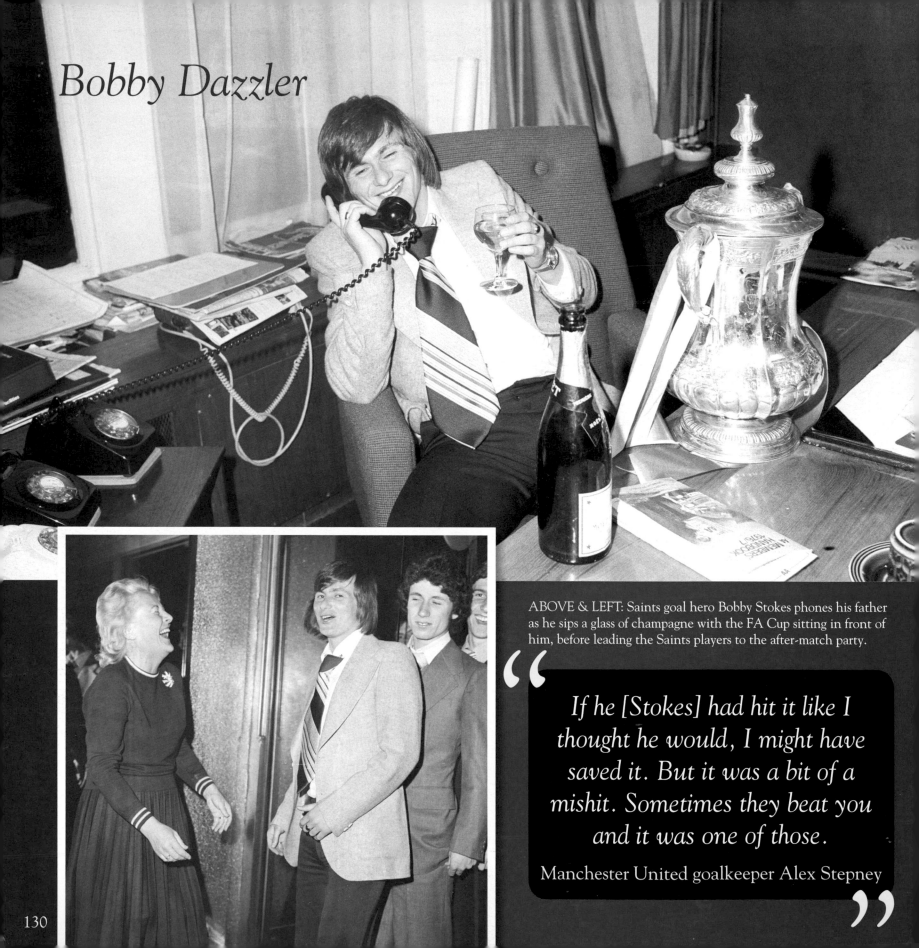

ABOVE & LEFT: Saints goal hero Bobby Stokes phones his father as he sips a glass of champagne with the FA Cup sitting in front of him, before leading the Saints players to the after-match party.

" *If he [Stokes] had hit it like I thought he would, I might have saved it. But it was a bit of a mishit. Sometimes they beat you and it was one of those.*

Manchester United goalkeeper Alex Stepney "

Secretary Keith Honey gets his hands on the FA Cup during the after-match bash at the Talk of the Town in London.

Victory Parade

The FA Cup winners are mobbed as the victory parade makes its way, albeit very slowly, through the streets of Southampton.

Over 250,000 people turned out to see their returning heroes on the Sunday morning. The bus even had to take a diversion via the Ford factory to prevent mass-absenteeism!

" *We were all shocked by the reception we got. We thought the parade would take half and hour, not half a day.* "

Nick Holmes

" *I'll never forget it. I don't believe any cup-winning team have had a homecoming like it.* "

David Peach

Any vantage point will do for these fans as they pack the town to get a glimpse of the FA Cup winners.

> " *It was our finest hour but not our finest team. That was the one I came back from Manchester City with the likes of Kevin Keegan and Alan Ball.* "
>
> Mick Channon

I'll drink to that. Lawrie McMenemy takes a swig from the old pot during the victory parade.

"It's the only major thing Southampton have ever won, and it was totally unexpected. That is why people in this area, whether they were Saints fans or not, enjoyed it so much. They didn't have to be football supporters, they all came out – more than 250,000 of them. The big clubs are expected to win a cup every now and again but with Southampton it was a special, special thing."

Lawrie McMenemy

Bobby Stokes was presented with a car at Mick Channon's testimonial after his final heroics. The only problem was the Southampton striker couldn't drive!

LAWRIE'S
–LEGENDS–

Ian Turner
Signed by Lawrie McMenemy from his former club Grimsby, Turner quit English football in 1978 at the age of 28, after a knee injury, to join Fort Lauderdale.

Peter Rodrigues
Experienced Welsh international full-back who joined Southampton from Sheffield Wednesday in 1975 and captained Saints at Wembley. Rodrigues said: "When I came out of the tunnel before the game I felt 100ft tall – it was an enormous atmosphere. At the end, my knees were shaking with delight knowing I would be collecting the Cup from the Queen which was one of the proudest moments of my life."

David Peach
A ballboy at the 1966 World Cup final, the left-back kept Steve Coppell quiet in the final and kept his cool to score a crucial spot kick in the last-four win over Palace.

Nick Holmes
Versatile and dependable, he played 543 league games for Saints between 1972 and 1987. Along with Peach, he was the only survivor of Saints' cup-winning side to return for the 1979 League Cup final.

Mel Blyth
Composed centre-back who made 105 league appearances, from 1974 to 1977, and later played in South Africa, the USA and Hong Kong.

Jim Steele
A trainee mechanical engineer for the National Coal Board before joining Dundee, Steele was a tough defender who signed for Saints for a club record fee of £80,000 in 1972.

Paul Gilchrist
This industrious frontman, who scored 17 goals in 107 games from 1972 to 1977, scored the all-important opening goal in the semi-final.

Mick Channon
Channon was instrumental within the team in the lead-up to Wembley and his experience was a crucial factor in the final. McMenemy remembers how horse-racing lover Channon phoned his room on the morning of the match. He said: "Being into betting, Mick said 'have you seen the odds?' We were 5/1 in a two-horse race – that's how unlikely we were to win it. I didn't bet on us – I never did – but whoever did, did very well."

Peter Osgood
A Chelsea legend, famous for his flamboyant lifestyle off the pitch, scored in every round when he won the cup with the Blues in 1970. Ossie joined Saints in 1974 and stayed for three years before a move to Philadelphia Fury and a brief spell back at Stamford Bridge.

Jim McCalliog
Intelligent midfielder who lost the 1966 Cup final with Sheffield Wednesday despite scoring the opener against Everton – but was a winner at Wembley a year later when he returned with Scotland to beat world champions England. Was sold by United boss Tommy Docherty to Southampton in 1975.

Bobby Stokes
Outstanding schoolboy who came through the ranks at The Dell, Stokes, known for his quick-fire wit, made just eight more full appearances for the Saints after the final, before stints with Washington Diplomats and Portsmouth.

Substitute: Hugh Fisher (unused)
Scored a vital late equalizer in the third round against Aston Villa – but an injury kept him on the bench at Wembley.

Manchester United's FA Cup final line-up: Stepney, Forsyth, Houston, Daly, Greenhoff, Buchan (capt), Coppell, McIlroy, Pearson, Macari and Hill.

Channon's Night

The party rolled into Mike Channon's testimonial on 3rd May against QPR. The FA Cup winners – and Channon – were in huge demand as a crowd of 29,000 crammed into The Dell to salute a legend.

Channon remembered the night fondly: "I had to be at The Dell early that day and found people had been queuing since six in the morning. It was a sell-out."

ABOVE: Fans spill on to the edge of the pitch as The Dell is packed to capacity.

BELOW: Mike Channon parades the FA Cup in front of the supporters as the Saints legend takes in the emotion of the night.

Euro Heartache

The second leg of the European Cup Winners' Cup third-round tie against Anderlecht on 16th March 1977 was one of the great European nights at The Dell.

The Belgians, a European powerhouse, and the Cup Winners' Cup holders and Super Cup champions at the time, were 2-0 up from the first leg in Brussels and the tie seemed a formality – but Saints went within seven minutes of forcing them into extra-time.

David Peach rattled the visitors after he scored from the penalty spot, and new signing Ted MacDougall levelled the tie to send the 24,337-strong crowd wild.

But François Van der Elst exploited a slip by Jim Steele and the European dream was cruelly ended. Anderlecht went on to the final, but lost 2-0 to German side SV Hamburg.

David Peach scores from the penalty spot to get Saints back into the game against Anderlecht in March 1977.

LEFT: Nick Holmes is devastated after François Van der Elst, who looks far from happy, scores the late winner for the Belgian giants.

BELOW: Mick Channon can't find a way through the Anderlecht defence at The Dell.

141

Peter Osgood (far left), Ted MacDougall, boss Lawrie McMenemy, Alan Ball and Mick Channon (far right) prepare to do battle with Manchester United in the FA Cup fifth round at The Dell, in a repeat of the previous year's final.

Manchester United snatched a 2-2 draw and won the replay 2-1 at Old Trafford in March 1977 to end Saints' brilliant 14-game unbeaten run in the cup – and their brave defence of the trophy. Tommy Docherty's men went on to lift the cup.

BELOW & BELOW INSET: Manchester United players and fans celebrate scoring at The Dell in the FA Cup fifth round. Such was the interest and magnitude of the tie around the town supporters sought to watch from any vantage point – including a tree!

August 1976: Lose 1-0 to Liverpool in the Charity Shield at Wembley. **September 1976:** A poor start to the season leaves Saints bottom of the Second Division after six games. **15th September 1976:** Marseille are thrashed 4-0 in the first leg of the Cup Winners' Cup first round at The Dell. Malcolm Waldron, Mick Channon and Steve Williams put Saints out of sight, and Channon bags his second and a fourth from the spot. **29th September 1976:** Although beaten 2-1 in the second leg, David Peach ends Marseille's hopes of a comeback with an all-important away goal, leading the French giants to resort to strong-arm tactics. The Saints' coach is stoned as the players leave the ground. **November 1976:** Saints hammer Northern Irish side Carrick Rangers 9-3 on aggregate in the Cup Winners' Cup second round. **22nd January 1977:** Beat Carlisle 6-0 at Brunton Park to record best-ever away win. **March 1977:** Knocked out of Cup Winners' Cup in third round by Anderlecht. **May 1977:** Finish in the top half, with Ted MacDougall scoring 23 goals and Mick Channon 17.

Having a Ball

BELOW: Alan Ball, signed by Lawrie McMenemy from Arsenal for £60,000 in December 1976, was one of the driving forces behind Southampton's return to the top flight. The World Cup winner was given the armband, and rewarded McMenemy with some magnificent performances during the 1977–78 campaign.

ABOVE: New signing Phil Boyer is restrained by Bolton defenders during the 2-2 draw at The Dell in October 1977. He was booked for retaliation, but also scored.

Saints Are Fizzing Again

Lawrie McMenemy pours champagne over goalscorer Tony Funnell after his header in the 1-1 draw against Leyton Orient sealed Southampton's return to the top flight in 1978.

But the season had begun on a sad note as Dell legend Mick Channon quit to join Manchester City for £300,000 in July 1977.

McMenemy quickly put the money to good use and signed Phil Boyer for £130,000; his partnership with Ted MacDougall quickly flourished as it had done at York, Bournemouth and Norwich before they linked up again at The Dell.

A 0-0 draw at The Dell against Spurs on the last day of the season allowed Bolton to pip the Saints to the title by a point.

RIGHT: The *Mirror* back page splashes with Southampton's promotion back to the First Division in 1978.

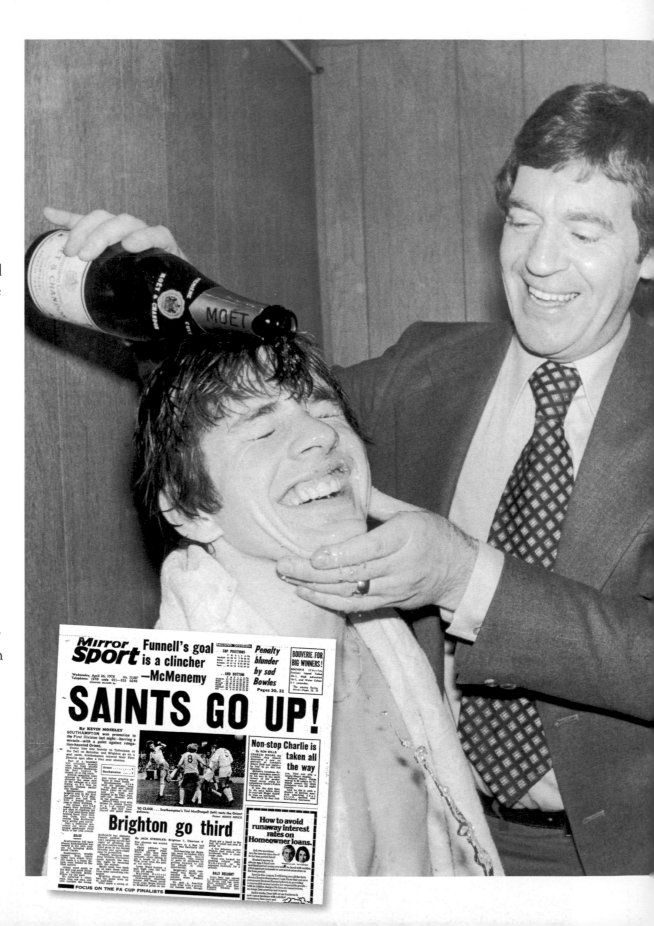

The Ted MacDougall (left) and Phil Boyer striking partnership again comes to fruition as they scored 31 goals between them in the promotion campaign.

–LEGENDS–

Lawrie McMenemy MBE

Lawrie McMenemy is the club's most successful manager. During his tenure, he won the FA Cup in 1976 and also reached the League Cup final in 1979, although they lost to Cloughie's Nottingham Forest. McMenemy pulled off one of the greatest transfer coups in the history of the club by signing then European Footballer of the Year, Kevin Keegan, from SV Hamburg in 1980. In 1984 he guided Saints to second place in the First Division – their highest-ever finish – and the FA Cup semi-final. McMenemy was also assistant manager to Graham Taylor during his England reign, and managed England Under-21s and Northern Ireland.

RIGHT: At home with the FA Cup in 1977.

BELOW: Billy Bingham, Bobby Robson, Terry Venables and Lawrie, among others, in a recording studio in March 1988.

FOOTBALL –STATS–

Lawrie McMenemy MBE

Name: Lawrie McMenemy
Date of Birth: 26th July 1936
Managerial Career:
Bishop Auckland (1965–67)
Doncaster (1968–71)
Grimsby (1971–73)
Southampton (1973–85)
Sunderland (1985–87)
England Under-21 (1990–93)
Northern Ireland (1998–99)

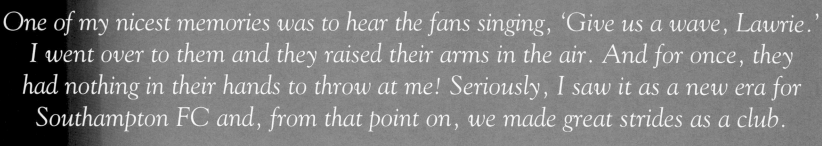

One of my nicest memories was to hear the fans singing, 'Give us a wave, Lawrie.' I went over to them and they raised their arms in the air. And for once, they had nothing in their hands to throw at me! Seriously, I saw it as a new era for Southampton FC and, from that point on, we made great strides as a club.

Lawrie McMenemy, after winning the FA Cup in 1976

BELOW INSET: Lawrie shares a joke with Paul Gascoigne before England's World Cup qualifier against Turkey in November 1992.

BELOW: Lawrie leads Saints out alongside Liverpool boss Bob Paisley for the 1976 Charity Shield.

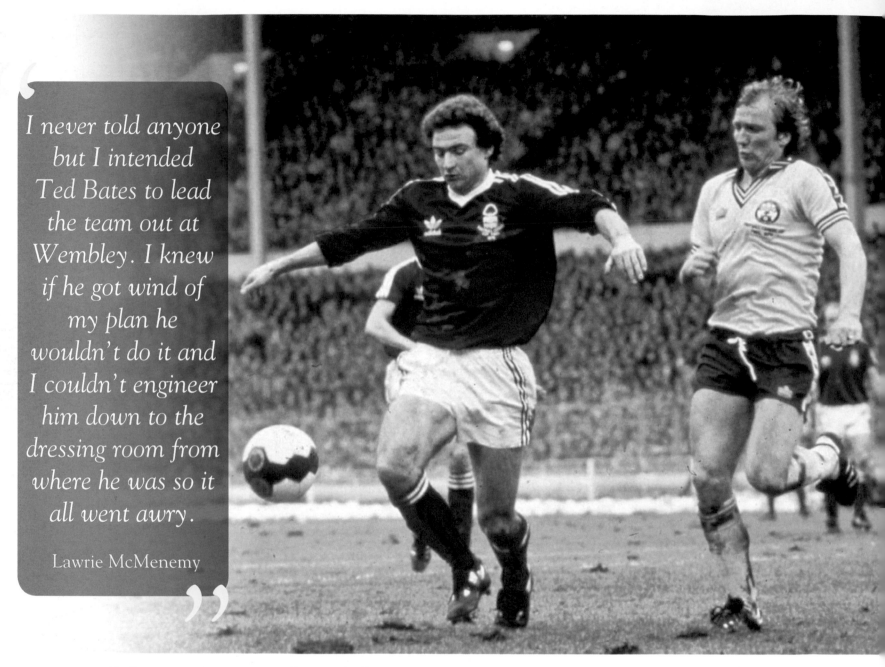

> *I never told anyone but I intended Ted Bates to lead the team out at Wembley. I knew if he got wind of my plan he wouldn't do it and I couldn't engineer him down to the dressing room from where he was so it all went awry.*
>
> Lawrie McMenemy

Wembley Heartbreak

Despite the glamour of their top-flight return, the highlight of the season was another brilliant cup run and Wembley final in 1979.

Here, David Peach battles with Nottingham Forest's Martin O'Neill as Southampton again wore their "lucky" yellow kit.

Peach put Southampton ahead but Forest hit back and, despite Nick Holmes scoring late in the game, Brian Clough's team won 3-2 – but Saints were far from disgraced as Forest went on to win the European Cup later in the year.

The loss of the cup did not seem to detract from the Saints' efforts and they finished 14th in the league – a comfortable 15 points above the relegation zone – although they found goals hard to come by, scoring just 47.

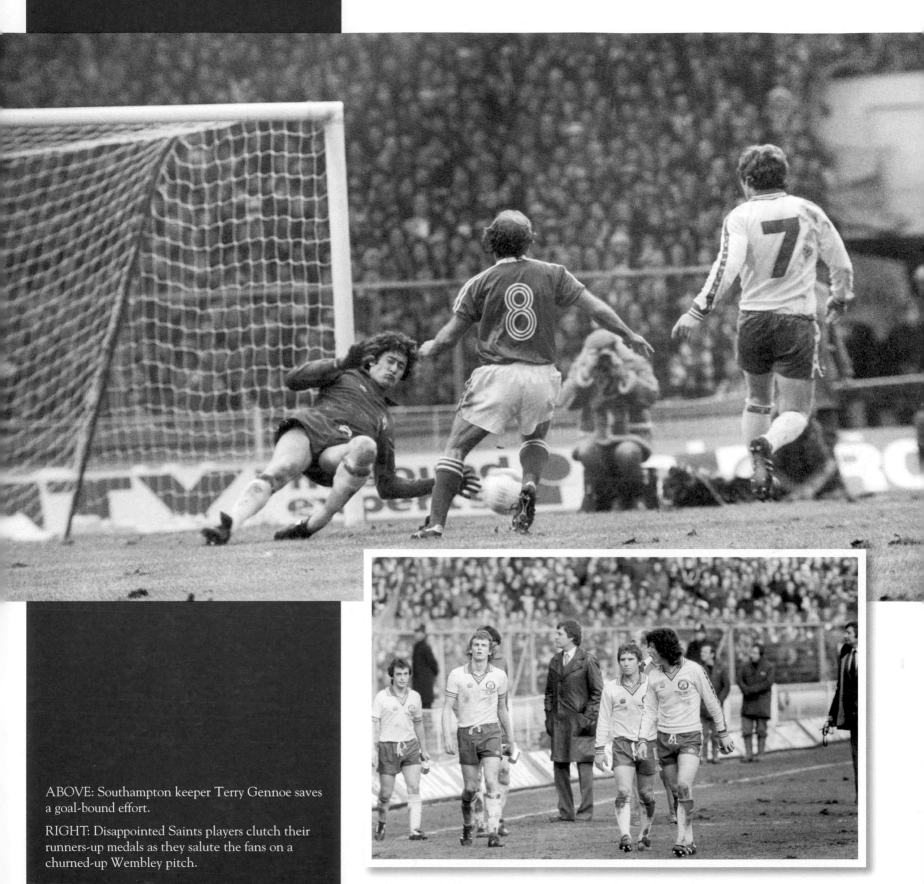

ABOVE: Southampton keeper Terry Gennoe saves a goal-bound effort.

RIGHT: Disappointed Saints players clutch their runners-up medals as they salute the fans on a churned-up Wembley pitch.

August 1979: After being scouted as schoolboy, Steve Moran is signed by Saints. **10th November 1979:** Saints get a little revenge on Nottingham Forest after their league final defeat with a 4-1 win at The Dell; Phil Boyer hits two. The mighty Forest, European champions at the time, had not conceded three goals or more in the league for over two years. **19th January 1980:** Steve Moran makes his debut as a substitute in the 4-1 win over Manchester City, scoring with his first touch of the ball. **May 1980:** Alan Ball departs to take up the post of player-manager at Blackpool.

Phil Boyer (on the ground) finished the 1979–80 season with a flourish and a third hat-trick of the season on the penultimate day in a 5-2 romp over Bristol City. He was the First Division top scorer, with 23 goals, as Saints finished eighth.

Boyer's return to form – he scored just seven goals during the 1978–79 campaign – coincided with the arrival of Mick Channon from Manchester City for £100,000 after he failed to settle at Maine Road.

ABOVE: Charlie George made his long-awaited home debut in the 1-1 draw with Manchester United in August 1979 after he was bought for £400,000 from Derby in October 1978. But injuries blighted his time at Southampton, none more so than when he lost his index finger after an accident with a lawnmower.

LEFT: Steve Williams had emerged as a cultured midfielder and was making a name for himself at The Dell. His England Under-21 debut came on the back of some fine performances in 1977 and he succeeded Alan Ball as captain in 1980.

Keegan Mania

In one of the greatest transfer coups ever seen, Lawrie McMenemy secured the services of European Footballer of the Year, Kevin Keegan.

The Saints boss called a press conference at the Potters Heron Hotel, Ampfield, in February 1980 to reveal the summer signing of Keegan from German giants SV Hamburg for £420,000 – but Keegan's first season was wrecked by injuries. Here, Keegan is carried down the touchline in front of worried Saints fans during the 2-1 home defeat to Aston Villa in October 1980. Despite King Kev missing 15 games through injury, Saints qualified for the UEFA Cup after finishing sixth – their highest ever place in the First Division – scoring 76 goals.

> "I got Kevin in a room and immediately locked the door. I told him about the club's plans and, after three hours talking, he had agreed to join us. Why did I lock the door? Well, I'm not as quick as I used to be and wanted to do everything in my power to get Kevin.
>
> Lawrie McMenemy

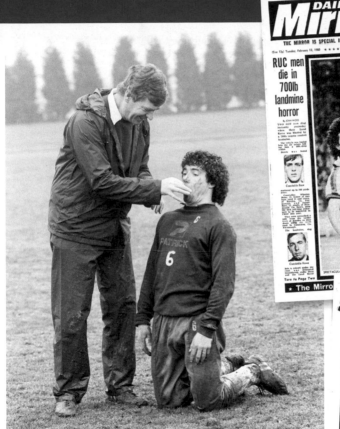

ABOVE: Lawrie McMenemy shares a joke with Kevin Keegan in training.

RIGHT: Kevin Keegan's return to English football with Southampton makes the *Mirror*'s front and back pages. Kevin Mosely gets the interview they all wanted as Big Lawrie revealed how he pulled off a transfer masterstroke.

ABOVE: Kevin Keegan leads Saints out on his return to Anfield in February 1981. He received a hero's welcome from the 41,575-strong crowd, but was on the end of a 2-0 defeat by his former club.

LEFT: Saints fans held their breath in June 1980 in hopes that England captain Kevin Keegan would come through the European Championships unscathed. Tackles like this in the 2-1 win over Spain will have made Lawrie McMenemy wince. The Three Lions failed to make it past the group stages and King Kev returned home fit to make his Southampton debut in August 1980 against Manchester City at The Dell.

September 1980: One of Southampton's worst ever displays as they are dumped out of the League Cup after extra-time at Vicarage Road. They are clobbered 7-1, having beaten the Hornets 4-0 in the first leg at The Dell a week earlier. **November 1980:** Phil Boyer joins Manchester City for £220,000. **March 1981:** Alan Ball returns to The Dell.

Kevin Keegan connects with a glancing header at Anfield as Graeme Souness and Alan Hansen (No.6) look on during Southampton's brilliant win in 1981.

LEFT: Steve Moran fends off an Aston Villa player in October 1980. Despite scoring in the game, Saints lost 2-1, but Moran went on to hit 18 goals in just 30 starts in the 1980–81 campaign.

BELOW: Danny Wallace – 16 years and 314 days old – became the youngest ever Saints player since the war in November 1980.

Saints boss Lawrie McMenemy finally landed the big one and shared the Head of the Year award in 1981 with Felicity Kendal.

161

September 1981: Kevin Keegan scores in the opening four games as David Armstrong, a £600,000 signing from Middlesbrough, pulls the strings in midfield.

May 1982: After the high of January and topping the table, Saints end the season on a low with a final-day drubbing at Arsenal, but still finish seventh and qualify for the UEFA Cup. Steve Moran, despite missing almost half the season due to injury, was voted PFA Young Player of the Year.

> *It would have been nicer to have won in more style but to score so late and not really give them time to reply was perfect.*
>
> Kevin Keegan

Top of the League

Saints produced a stunning performance against one of the great Liverpool teams – who eventually won the title – to pull off the result of the season in late November 1981 at Anfield.

Steve Moran scored the winner three minutes from time and Saints went top of the First Division for the first time in their history on 30th January 1982 after a 1-0 win at Middlesbrough.

Lawrie McMenemy said: "It was like winning the cup all over again. It's the ambition of every club to go top of the league and to do it in January is no mean achievement. Nothing could take away how good we felt that day at Middlesbrough."

ABOVE: Proud dad Kevin Keegan cuddles his newborn daughter Sarah Marie in the Princess Anne Hospital, Southampton, in June 1982.

The Saints star made it a treble celebration as he was voted PFA Player of the Year and club Player of the Year.

LEFT: Comedian Freddie Starr plants a big smacker on Kevin Keegan as Elton John looks on. Southampton star Keegan was collecting the Golden Boot for his 26 goals in the 1981–82 league campaign.

Peter Shilton, here with Bryan Robson during the 1-1 draw with Manchester United at Old Trafford in April 1983, was signed for £300,000 from Nottingham Forest in August 1982. His capture was the only silver lining as the 1982–83 league campaign got off to a wretched start.

Mick Channon had left for a second time in the summer – and Kevin Keegan sensationally quit for Newcastle just days before the season started.

With Saints at the foot of the table, Alan Ball joined the exodus and signed for Hong Kong side Eastern Athletic in October 1982. Oddly, all these departures coincided with an upturn in Southampton's form and Lawrie McMenemy's side began to climb the table.

Saints pay him £100,000 — and £2,000 a week

GOLDEN MOVE FOR SHILTON

By DAVID MOORE

ABOVE: Peter Shilton signs for Southampton after talks with Forest boss Brian Clough broke down, say the *Mirror*.

By May 1983, some bright young talent had emerged. Mark Wright, Danny Wallace, Reuben Agboola and Steve Moran – who bagged a hat-trick against Manchester City – showed maturity beyond their years and repaid McMenemy's faith to secure a mid-table finish.

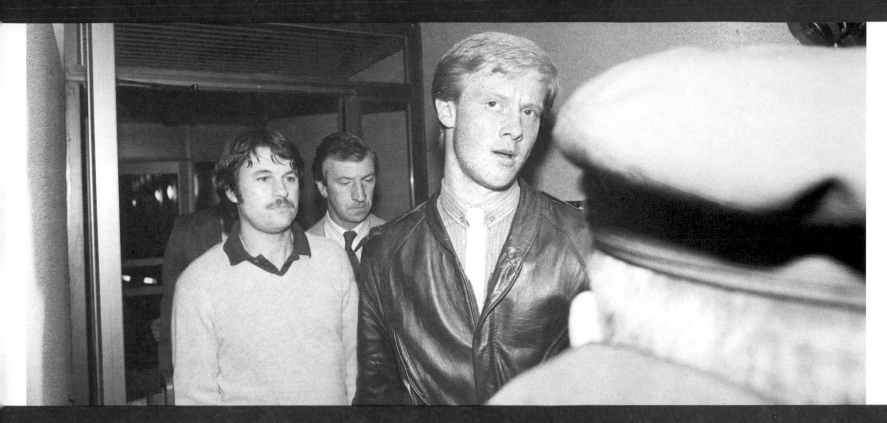

The UEFA Cup provided little respite for the beleaguered Saints as they succumbed to Norrköping on away goals in September 1982. To make matters worse, Steve Moran and Mark Wright were detained by Swedish police after a girl made accusations against them, which were later found to be untrue.

Pride of Hampshire

Portsmouth 0-1 Southampton
(FA Cup fourth round, 28th January 1984)

This will go down as one of the greatest south coast derbies in history – and the pivotal point in another brilliant FA Cup run for Saints.

Southampton were at the peak of their powers and on the fringes of the 1984 First Division title race while Portsmouth – after years in the doldrums – were moving in the right direction and were back in the Second Division.

Pompey were no pushovers and the Fratton Park factor also levelled the playing field in this fourth-round tie on 28th January but, ironically, Portsmouth were undone by the behaviour of their own crowd as Saints scored a dramatic injury-time winner.

David Armstrong's cross evaded goalkeeper Alan Knight, allowing Steve Moran to tap it in at the far post. Three extra minutes had been added after Saints left-back Mark Dennis had been hit by a coin while taking a throw-in.

"We've got a good result," laughed Lawrie McMenemy, "£4.50 in small change and 2lb of bananas." (The bananas had been thrown at Rueben Agboola.)

"Pompey had earned a replay. I don't think anybody in my dressing room would argue with that."

I've never seen a team quite so gutted as Portsmouth.

Lawrie McMenemy

Southampton players mob Steve Moran after his late winner as 36,000 fans crammed into Fratton Park using every vantage point possible. As the picture shows, fencing around the grounds was still very much in vogue in 1984 to combat the threat of crowd trouble that blighted the English game.

The Joke's On Soccer

Don't blame the thugs

ABOVE: Saints match-winner Steve Moran watches as Mark Hateley gets the better of Saints defender Mark Wright.

LEFT: Mark Dennis refuses to blame the Pompey fans after he was hit by a coin in the FA Cup tie at Fratton Park, according to the *Mirror*.

The Nearly Men

The 1983–84 season promised so much for so long but, ultimately, delivered nothing.

Danny Wallace's stunning double to secure a 2-0 win over Liverpool – whose team included Mark Lawrenson, Ronnie Whelan, Alan Hansen, Kenny Dalglish, Ian Rush and Steve Nicol – in front of the TV cameras on a magical night at The Dell in March 1984 announced Southampton's arrival in the title race.

And, with another brilliant FA Cup run unfolding, the Double was a real possibility. But, in the FA Cup semi-final at Highbury in April, a sickening blow was delivered by Everton's Adrian Heath in the 117th minute of extra-time, which again crushed Southampton's cup dream.

Although Lawrie McMenemy picked his side up, despite winning six of their last 10 games they were pipped to the title by Liverpool. Steve Moran led the goalscoring stakes with 21 league goals, while David Armstrong hit 15 and Danny Wallace 11.

1983–84 First Division top six

	P	W	D	L	F	A	Pts
Liverpool	42	22	14	6	73	32	80
Southampton	42	22	11	9	66	38	77
N Forest	42	22	8	12	76	45	74
Man United	42	20	14	8	71	41	74
QPR	42	22	7	13	67	37	73
Arsenal	42	18	9	15	74	60	63

LEFT: Danny Wallace is the toast of Southampton as they blow the title race wide open, according to the *Mirror*, in March 1984.

Danny Wallace wheels away in delight after his header made sure of the points against Liverpool at The Dell in March 1984.

The end of the 1983–84 season turned into the Danny Wallace show. He hit a hat-trick in the 8-2 hammering of Coventry and then bagged a double as Saints beat Tottenham 5-0.

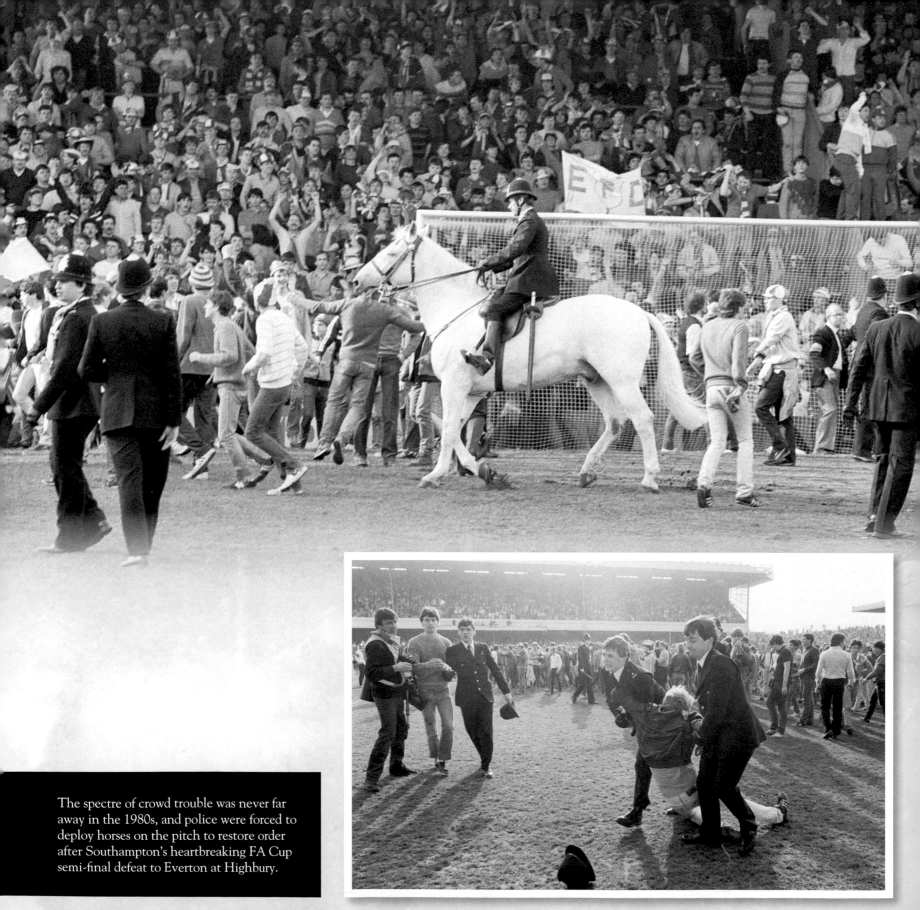

The spectre of crowd trouble was never far away in the 1980s, and police were forced to deploy horses on the pitch to restore order after Southampton's heartbreaking FA Cup semi-final defeat to Everton at Highbury.

Neville Southall and Kevin Ratcliffe appeal for calm after Adrian Heath's late goal in the FA Cup semi-final had led to a pitch invasion; the Everton match-winner is mobbed by jubilant Toffees fans.

Saints and Sinners

Steve Williams, Peter Shilton and Mark Wright all played in England's 1-0 win over East Germany at Wembley in September 1984 – a proud moment for the club and Saints fans.

But the 1984–85 campaign proved to be the straw that broke the camel's back as some unsavoury off-the-pitch antics marred the season.

Reuben Agboola was involved in an incident at a nightclub, while Williams and Wright publically criticized Lawrie McMenemy – and the ramifications were severe.

Agboola was offloaded to Sunderland, captain Williams was sold to Arsenal for a club record £550,000 and Wright, who at one point went on strike, was dropped by England.

With Williams unloaded to Arsenal, McMenemy brought in Jimmy Case from Brighton for £30,000 to bolster the midfield. It turned out to be his last signing for the club as Saints finished fifth despite their off-field distractions.

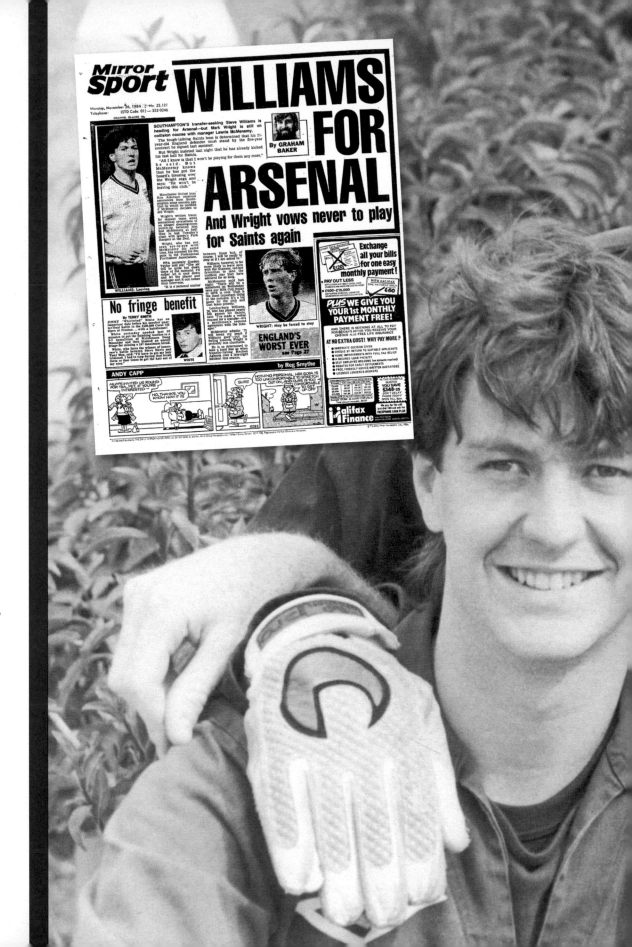

175

When FOOTBALL *Was* FOOTBALL

Fall and Rise of the Saints
1985-2012

> " Just 48 hours before I entered the unemployment statistics we got whipped at The Dell courtesy of one 18-year-old called Matthew Le Tissier.
>
> Ron Atkinson, after Le Tissier had taken his Manchester United side apart in November 1986 "

June 1985: Lawrie McMenemy drops a bombshell and quits The Dell, bringing to a close the finest era the club has ever seen. Five days later, he is unveiled as Sunderland manager. **August 1985:** Chris Nicholl is appointed manager. **October 1985:** An indifferent start to the season hits rock bottom with a 7-0 hammering by Luton at Kenilworth Road – and a relegation battle looks to be on the cards. **November 1985:** Everton ruin Southampton's centenary party with a 3-2 win at The Dell. **January 1986:** Danny Wallace hits a hat-trick in the FA Cup third-round win against Middlesbrough at Ayresome Park. It's the first treble by a Saints player in an away FA Cup tie since Derek Reeves' in 1960. **May 1986:** Despite two heavy defeats at the end of the season (6-1 at Everton and 5-3 at Spurs), Saints survive – but it's their worst league finish for years.

Wright Agony

Mark Wright lies in agony with a broken leg after a collision with Peter Shilton and Craig Johnson during the 2-0 FA Cup semi-final defeat to Liverpool at White Hart Lane in April 1986. After a goalless 90 minutes, Ian Rush struck twice in the first half of extra-time for the Merseysiders.

Ian Rush slots the ball past Peter Shilton to put Liverpool into the FA Cup final.

RIGHT: Joe Jordan wins this header in front of a very sparse crowd at Stamford Bridge in September 1985. Just 16,711 turned up to see Chelsea beat Saints 2-0 – an unthinkable prospect today. But life after Lawrie was proving tough at The Dell as league performances dipped, and things began to fall apart off the pitch too.

Summer 1986: Chris Nicholl signs Bournemouth's Colin Clarke for £400,000, but the £300,000 sale of Steve Moran to Leicester City raises a few eyebrows. **August 1986:** Colin Clarke hits a hat-trick on the opening day in a 5-1 win over QPR and scores another treble at the beginning of October against Newcastle. **4th November 1986:** Eighteen-year-old Matthew Le Tissier scores his first goal for the club just 75 seconds after coming on in the League Cup third-round replay against Manchester United, which Saints won 4-1. **8th November 1986:** Matthew Le Tissier gets his first league goal in the 3-1 defeat at Sheffield Wednesday. **February 1987:** Liverpool beat Saints over two legs in the Littlewoods Cup semi-final. **August 1987:** Mark Wright moves to Derby for £760,000, a club record fee, and Peter Shilton joins him in the East Midlands.

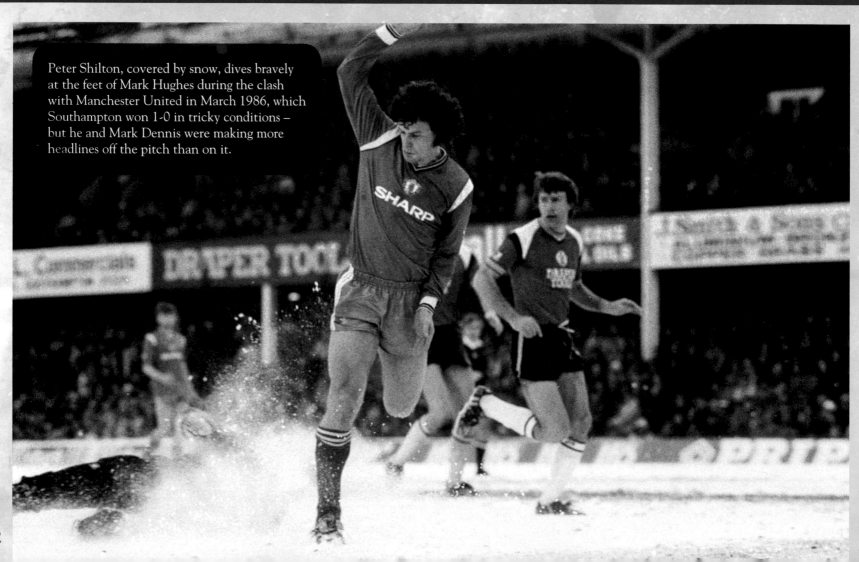

Peter Shilton, covered by snow, dives bravely at the feet of Mark Hughes during the clash with Manchester United in March 1986, which Southampton won 1-0 in tricky conditions – but he and Mark Dennis were making more headlines off the pitch than on it.

Hitting the Wrong Headlines

LEFT: The *Mirror*'s front page reveals that Peter Shilton has been arrested after a bust-up with his wife in December 1986.

RIGHT: Mark Dennis is banned for seven days by Southampton after a punch-up with Peter Shilton.

LEFT: Mark Dennis lifts the lid on his bitter feud with Peter Shilton in December 1986.

RIGHT: The *Mirror* back page makes a big splash with the ugly dressing room bust-up between manager Chris Nicholl and Mark Dennis in February 1987. It eventually led to Dennis getting sacked.

Nick Holmes relaxes in the bath after Saints had beaten Crystal Palace in the 1976 FA Cup semi-final.

–LEGENDS–

Nick Holmes

Lawrie McMenemy praised his "reliability, dependability and flexibility", adding that he was "a man for all seasons". Holmes was an ever-present player when Southampton finished second in the First Division in the 1983–84 season, and was part of a midfield that was probably the best in the club's history. But a pelvic injury forced him to retire in May 1987.

He may have been a Wembley loser in the 1979 League Cup final, but Nick Holmes did get on the scoresheet.

FOOTBALL –STATS–

Nick Holmes

Name: Nick Holmes
Date of Birth: 11th November 1954
Position: Defender/midfielder
Playing Career: Southampton (1972–87)
Southampton Appearances: 444
Southampton Goals: 56
Managerial Career: Salisbury City (2002–10)
England Caps: 0

Jaw Dropper

Glenn Cockerill recovers at home with his children after he was punched by Arsenal and England star Paul Davis during the 2-2 draw at Highbury in September 1988. The horror attack left Cockerill needing an operation; he had to have a metal plate inserted into his jaw, which was broken in two places. Executed off the ball, the punch was missed by the referee and his linesmen. But, in the first example of the use of video evidence by the disciplinary authorities, the television footage was enough for the FA to suspend Davis for nine matches, accompanied by a record £3,000 fine.

> " *I'd been having a running verbal battle with Paul Davis throughout the game. I didn't think it was anything too serious. Then, suddenly, there was the punch.* "
>
> Glenn Cockerill

May 1991: Chris Nicholl is sacked as manager. His departure heralds 20 years of managerial mayhem. June 1991: Ian Branfoot is appointed in June. Saints make a wretched start but avoid relegation. 15th August 1992: First game in the new Sky Sports-backed Premiership ends in a 0-0 draw with Tottenham at The Dell. 19th August 1992: Matthew Le Tissier scores Saints' first ever goal in the new league in a 3-1 defeat to QPR. 28th August 1992: Saints' 2-1 victory over Middlesbrough is their first Premiership win. May 1993: Southampton finish 18th, one point above the drop zone, and relegation battles become the shape of things to come through the 1990s.

Shear Class

Alan Shearer hit a 49-minute hat-trick in the 4-2 victory over Arsenal at The Dell on 9th April 1988 on his full debut. Shearer, at 17 years and 240 days old, became the youngest ever player to score a top-flight treble.

But Gunners boss George Graham was less than generous saying: "It would have been different if Adams and O'Leary had been playing. Shearer would not have got his goals so easily."

> *I don't think I realised the enormity of what I had done.*
>
> Alan Shearer

Hardman Neil "Razor" Ruddock was never one to shirk a challenge and he lets Peter Beardsley know he's about as Rod Wallace closes in. Saints made a good start to the 1989–90 campaign, and another ding-dong battle with Liverpool in October at The Dell was a real treat for the fans. The emergence of Tim Flowers, Matthew Le Tissier, Wallace and Jason Dodd, the latter making his debut, were proof the club were heading in the right direction after the turmoil and off-field problems of the previous campaign, and a 4-1 win set the tone for the season as they finished seventh and hit 71 goals.

> " On the day of the match there was me, Le Tiss, Barry Horne and Micky Adams all eating in McDonald's a couple of hours before kick-off. The unusual preparations didn't do us too badly and we put on our best performance of the season. "
>
> Neil Ruddock

ABOVE: Rod Wallace (centre), scorer of two goals, gives Francis Benali reason to celebrate as beleaguered Liverpool players prepare for the restart. Rod made history with his brothers – Danny and Ray – in October 1988 when they all played for Saints against Sheffield Wednesday at The Dell. It was the first time three brothers had lined up for the same team in the top flight.

LEFT: Matthew Le Tissier picks up the PFA Young Player of the Year for his 24 goals in the 1989–90 campaign.

Matthew Le Tissier scores in the 3-1 FA Cup third-round win at Tottenham in 1990. Such was his mercurial talent, Le Tissier almost single-handedly kept Southampton in the top flight through the 1990s. And even when bigger clubs such as Tottenham and Chelsea came knocking, he stayed loyal to Southampton.

January 1994: Ian Branfoot is sacked after a disastrous tenure. Alan Ball is appointed and Matthew Le Tissier becomes his talisman. **March 1994:** Matthew Le Tissier comes on as substitute to make his England debut. The Three Lions beat Denmark 1-0 at Wembley. **May 1994:** Southampton draw 3-3 on the final day at West Ham to stay up. Matthew Le Tissier hit 25 league goals. **May 1995:** Saints finish 10th. Matthew Le Tissier scores 25 league goals. **Summer 1995:** Alan Ball quits for Manchester City and Dave Merrington takes charge. **April 1996:** Saints beat Manchester United 3-1 at The Dell in the infamous game where Sir Alex Ferguson's men were wearing the "wrong colour shirts". **May 1996:** A 0-0 draw with Wimbledon at The Dell during the final preserves Saints' top-fight status. **June 1996:** Graeme Souness replaces the sacked Dave Merrington. **26th October 1996:** Despite another season of struggles, the 6-3 hammering of Manchester United at The Dell offers the fans some respite. **December 1996:** Rupert Lowe succeeds Guy Askham as chairman. The club's parent company, Southampton Leisure Holdings, is floated on the stock market. **May 1997:** Saints lose 1-0 on the final day at Villa Park but, with other results going their way, again avoid relegation – this time by one point.

Lawrie McMenemy returned to The Dell as a director in December 1993, when the club was struggling to preserve their top-flight status. The former Saints boss had taken up the post of England's assistant manager, under Graham Taylor, and watches glumly from the bench during the defeat to Spain in Santander in 1992.

May 1997: Graeme Souness and Lawrie McMenemy resign, citing "difficulties with the new owners". Dave Jones is Saints' fifth manager in five seasons. April 1998: Matthew Le Tissier scores a hat-trick for England B against Russia B at Loftus Road. Despite starring in the 4-1 win, he is left out of the England 1998 World Cup squad. May 1999: Saints take their top-flight survival to the final day again, but a 2-0 win at home to Everton ensures their safety.

Blooming Flowers

If not the result of the 1991–92 campaign, the celebration of the season. Tim Flowers ran the length of the Old Trafford pitch to celebrate with the Saints fans after his penalty shoot-out heroics. The FA Cup fourth-round tie had finished goalless at The Dell and extra-time could not separate the sides in the replay. Flowers saw to it that Saints pulled off a massive shock win as he saved Ryan Giggs' decisive penalty.

RIGHT: Tim Flowers wins the tie for Southampton with this penalty save from Ryan Giggs.

> " *Timmy just stood up and saved Giggs's penalty and he set off down the touchline with Glenn Cockerill chasing him. It was a cracking night.* "
>
> Matthew Le Tissier

BELOW: Matthew Le Tissier and Iain Dowie congratulate hero Tim Flowers after Saints beat Manchester United on penalties in the FA Cup at Old Trafford.

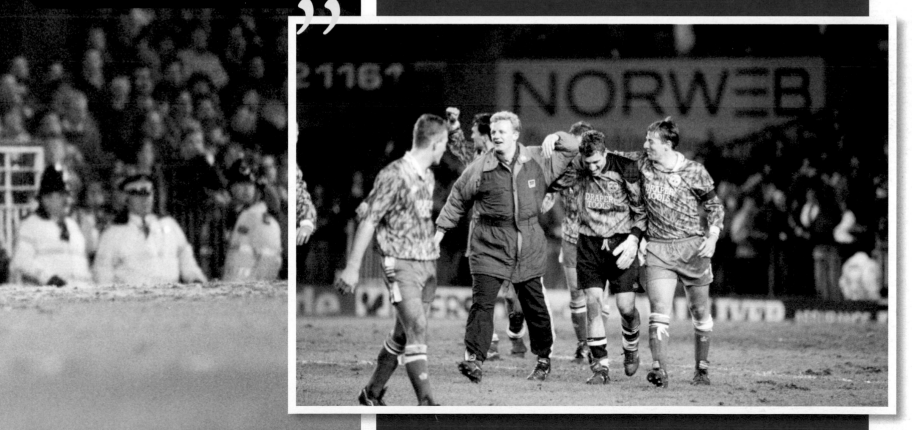

July 1999: Dean Richards joins on a free from Wolves. **December 1999:** Construction begins on the new stadium at St Mary's. **January 2000:** No sooner have things started to settle down on the pitch, Dave Jones is placed on "gardening leave" to concentrate on child sex charges brought against him. Glenn Hoddle takes charge. **April 2000:** Matthew Le Tissier scores his 100th Premiership goal, making him only the sixth player at the time, and the first midfielder, to reach this milestone. **May 2000:** Finish 15th place, 11 points above the relegation spot. **December 2000:** Dave Jones is not reinstated as manager, despite being cleared of all sex charges, and Hoddle continues as manager. **March 2001:** Again Saints are plunged into turmoil as Glenn Hoddle defects to Spurs. Stuart Gray takes charge. **19th May 2001:** A historic and emotional day as Saints beat Arsenal 3-2 in the last ever league game at The Dell. Fittingly, Matthew Le Tissier scores the final league goal at the old ground with two minutes remaining – and it turns out to be his last for the club.

Kevin Moore scored Southampton's first goal in the 1992 Zenith Data Systems Cup final at Wembley but Ian Branfoot's side were beaten 3-2 after extra-time by Nottingham Forest.

A sight football fans have got used to seeing down the years. Alan Shearer powers a header towards goal at Wembley.

BELOW: Ian Branfoot (sitting, in the blue coat) did not impress Saints purists with his style of play, and the early 1990s were underpinned with bad performances and poor team selections. On the far right here, Brian Clough and Stuart Pearce watch from the Forest bench.

–LEGENDS–

Matthew Le Tissier

Affectionately known as "Le God" by the Saints fans, Le Tissier's brilliance kept the club in the top flight through the 1990s. Lethal from dead-ball situations, he was the best penalty taker in the country – he converted 47 of the 48 penalties he took for the club. Nottingham Forest keeper Mark Crossley saved the one that got away in March 1993. Le Tissier could have moved on to bigger and better things but remained loyal to Southampton. He now works as a pundit on *Soccer Saturday*.

> *His talent was out of the norm. He could simply dribble past seven or eight players but without speed – he just walked past them. For me, he was sensational.*
>
> Barcelona star Xavi

FOOTBALL –STATS–

Matthew Le Tissier

Name: Matthew Le Tissier

Date of Birth: 14th October 1968

Position: Midfielder

Playing Career: Southampton (1986–2002)

Southampton Appearances: 443

Southampton Goals: 162

England Caps: 8

1st August 2001: Saints open new 32,000-capacity St Mary's Stadium with a 3-2 friendly defeat against Spanish side Espanyol. **September 2001:** Dean Richards is sold to Spurs for £8.1 million. **October 2001:** Saints lose six of their first eight games and Stuart Gray is sacked. Gordon Strachan is appointed manager. **24th October 2001:** Marian Pahars scores the first Saints league goal at St Mary's in the 3-1 defeat to Aston Villa. **24th November 2001:** Saints win at their new home at the sixth time of asking with a 1-0 victory over Charlton. **30th January 2002:** Matthew Le Tissier makes his last competitive appearance for Saints in a 2-0 win over West Ham. **March 2002:** Matthew Le Tissier announces his retirement. **May 2002:** Finish 11th. Matthew Le Tissier's testimonial – a 9-9 draw against an England XI – is watched by 31,904 fans. **May 2003:** James Beattie ends the season third in the Premier League scoring charts with 23 goals – and as top English marksman – as Saints finished eighth.

Southampton have provided the England team with some great players down the years and none more so than Alan Shearer. He is pictured with David Hirst and Gary Lineker in February 1992 shortly before his big move to Blackburn for a British record fee of £3.3 million. But Saints failed to insert a buy-on clause in the deal and it proved costly as, four years later, Shearer was sold to Newcastle for a then world record fee of £15 million. He went on to captain England and is the Premier League's all-time leading scorer.

August 2003: Beaten in the UEFA Cup first round by Steaua Bucharest. **February 2004:** Gordon Strachan quits, citing "personal reasons", and Steve Wigley is put in temporary charge. **March 2004:** Paul Sturrock is installed after guiding Plymouth to two promotions in three seasons. **May 2004:** Finish 12th as James Beattie scores 14 league goals. **August 2004:** Paul Sturrock leaves "by mutual consent" after just five months in charge and is replaced by Steve Wigley. **December 2004:** Steve Wigley's tenure proves equally disastrous and he is relieved of his duties as Saints languish in the relegation zone. **May 2005:** A 2-1 defeat to Manchester United at St Mary's ends Southampton's 27-year spell in the top flight as they finish bottom of the table. **December 2005:** George Burley is appointed as head coach to work alongside Sir Clive Woodward. **17th April 2006:** Gareth Bale makes his debut against Millwall, aged 16 years and 275 days, to become the second youngest ever Saints player. **May 2006:** Finish 12th in the Championship. Gareth Bale makes an international debut for Wales.

Wonder Wal

Alan Ball puts a young Theo Walcott through his paces at Southampton. He quickly made his mark at St Mary's with some fine youth team performances, and his substitute appearance in the 0-0 Championship draw at home to Wolves made him the youngest ever first-team player at 16 years and 143 days old.

Walcott also scored on his full senior debut at Elland Road on 18th October 2005. His rapid rise to fame was completed with a £9.1 million move to Arsenal in January 2006. Walcott's selection for the 2006 World Cup squad raised some eyebrows, but it persuaded Arsène Wenger to give him his Gunners bow on the first day of the 2006–07 campaign.

" *You would need a pistol to stop him.*

Pep Guardiola "

June 2006: Rupert Lowe resigns and is replaced as chairman by Jersey-based businessman Michael Wilde. February 2007: Michael Wilde stands down. March 2007: Leon Crouch takes on the role of acting chairman. May 2007: Saints lose on penalties to Derby in the Championship play-off semi-finals. July 2007: Leon Crouch is removed from the board but remains PLC director. February 2008: George Burley takes the Scotland national job and Nigel Pearson is installed in his place until the end of the season. May 2008: Saints stay up on the last day of the season. August 2008: Nigel Pearson's contract is not renewed and unknown Dutchman Jan Poortvliet is appointed head coach. January 2009: Jan Poortvliet resigns and fellow Dutchman Mark Wotte takes over.

" *I couldn't have asked any more from the players.* "

Gordon Strachan

Millennium Magic

With Gordon Strachan providing some much-needed stability to the club on and off the field, Saints fans at last had a reason for optimism.

The former Coventry manager, who may not have been many fans' first choice after Stuart Gray's sacking, masterminded a fine cup run to the final in 2003.

BELOW: Southampton chairman Rupert Lowe made his boldest move when he appointed Harry Redknapp, who had resigned as Pompey boss days earlier, as manager in December 2004. Redknapp took Saints down and, after a poor start to life in the Championship, defected back to Fratton Park in December 2005. The *Mirror* covered it all the way.

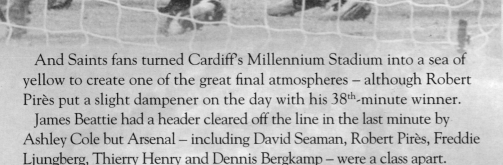

And Saints fans turned Cardiff's Millennium Stadium into a sea of yellow to create one of the great final atmospheres – although Robert Pirès put a slight dampener on the day with his 38th-minute winner.

James Beattie had a header cleared off the line in the last minute by Ashley Cole but Arsenal – including David Seaman, Robert Pirès, Freddie Ljungberg, Thierry Henry and Dennis Bergkamp – were a class apart.

Back in the Big Time

April 2009: Club's parent company Southampton Leisure Holdings goes into administration. Given a 10-point deduction and relegated to League One. **July 2009:** Administrators confirm club has been sold to billionaire Markus Liebherr. Alan Pardew is appointed manager. **March 2010:** Alex Oxlade-Chamberlain makes his Saints debut at the age of 16 years, 199 days. Apart from Theo Walcott he is the youngest player to appear in the first team, and he follows Walcott to Arsenal in August 2011 for £12 million. Saints beat Carlisle 4-1 in the Johnstone's Paint Trophy game at Wembley. **August 2010:** Owner Marcus Liebherr dies of a heart attack at the age of 62. Alan Pardew is sacked amid rumours he is in talks with Premier League side Newcastle. **12th September 2010:** Scunthorpe boss Nigel Adkins succeeds Pardew. **May 2011:** A 3-1 victory over Walsall seals promotion back to the Championship. **March 2012:** Rickie Lambert is named Championship Player of the Season. **April 2012:** Saints are promoted to the Premier League after beating Coventry on the final day of the season at St Mary's.

RIGHT: Saints are back in the top flight after a seven-year absence. Neil Adkins' side did not drop outside of the top two all season and were pipped to the title by a point by Reading. Rickie Lambert was top scorer again with 27 league goals.

10 Monday, April 30, 2012 — *In association with* VAUXHALL

CHAMPIONSHIP: SOU

SOUTHAMPTON: Davis 7, Butterfield 6, Hooiveld 7, Fonte 8, Fox 6, Schneiderlin 7, Hammond 5 (Cork 37, 8), Do Prado 8, Lallana 7 (Puncheon 83)
COVENTRY: Murphy 5, Baker 6, Hussey 5, Crainie 5, Clarke 5, Norwood 7, Thomas 5, Bigirimana 5 (Jeffers 46, 5), McSheffrey 6 (Roberts 34, 5), M

CHAMPIONSHIP

	P	W	D	L	F	A	Pts
Reading (C)	46	27	8	11	69	41	89
South'pton (P)	46	26	10	10	85	46	88
West Ham	46	24	14	8	81	48	86
Birmingham	46	20	16	10	78	51	76
Blackpool	46	20	15	11	79	59	75
Cardiff	46	19	18	9	66	53	75
Midd'brough	46	18	16	12	52	51	70
Hull	46	19	11	16	47	44	68
Leicester	46	18	12	16	66	55	66
Brighton	46	17	15	14	52	52	66
Watford	46	16	16	14	56	64	64
Derby	46	18	10	18	50	58	64
Burnley	46	17	11	18	61	58	62
Leeds	46	17	10	19	65	68	61
Ipswich	46	17	10	19	69	77	61
Millwall	46	15	12	19	55	57	57
C Palace	46	13	17	16	46	51	56
Peterboro	46	13	11	22	67	77	50
Nottm For	46	14	8	24	48	63	50
Bristol City	46	12	13	21	44	68	49
Barnsley	46	13	9	24	49	74	48
Por'mouth (R)	46	13	11	22	50	59	40
Coventry (R)	46	9	13	24	41	65	40
Doncaster (R)	46	8	12	26	43	80	36

BEAU
Promotion provides fitti

UP AND DOWNS

npower CHAMPIONSHIP

CHAMPIONSHIP:
Reading *champions*
Southampton *promoted*
Portsmouth, Coventry and Doncaster *relegated*

West Ham, Birmingham, Blackpool and Cardiff will contest the play-offs.

npower LEAGUE 1

LEAGUE ONE:
Charlton *champions*
Wycombe, Chesterfield, Exeter and Rochdale *relegated*

Sheff Wed will be promoted automatically if their final day result is at least as good as Sheff Utd's. One Sheffield club will join MK Dons and Huddersfield in the play-offs. Stevenage, Notts County and Carlisle will fight it out for the remaining play-off spot.

npower LEAGUE 2

LEAGUE TWO:
Swindon *champions*
Shrewsbury *promoted*
Macclesfield *relegated*

Crawley will be promoted if their result is at least as good as Torquay and Southend's. Two from Crawley, Torquay and Southend will join Cheltenham in the play-offs. Crewe will fill the remaining play-off spot providing they do not lose and Oxford win. Hereford must win to stay up and also hope Barnet do not win.

By MIKE WALTERS

BILLY SHARP'S triumphal procession into the promised land with Southampton is a happy ending for all of football to celebrate.

After a season punctuated by unimaginable tragedy and his escape from the madhouse of a club in thrall to a deluded agent, nobody deserved to cross the Premier League checkpoint more than Sharp.

Six months after cradling his dying son Luey, born scarcely 48 hours earlier, in a children's hospice with Match of the Day on TV in the background, Sharp found a measure of solace in Saints' going-up party.

Pitch invasions normally send players diving for cover, but Sharp and Adam Lallana became the promotion heroes who rushed ON to the field so they could be engulfed by the tide of jubilation.

Substituted before the carnival turned nuclear, they defied convention by charging from the dugout to join the revels, making the return journey by the rock stars' preferred mode of transport – crowd-surfing.

And by the time he had returned backstage, after joining his team-mates in the directors' box for an encore, Sharp was standing in his black underpants because he had given away his shorts to a fan as a 70th birthday present.

Seldom, if ever, has there been a more deserving candidate for promotion. Or the thinking man's choice as Footballer of the Year. Three days after every parent's worst nightmare last October, Sharp scored for Doncaster with a sumptuous, dipping volley against Middlesbrough and unveiled the T-shirt tribute: "That's for you son."

His £1.8million switch to Southampton was merciful release from Donny's nutty experiment of allowing agent Willie McKay to assemble a side of mercenary cast-offs.

Sharp, whose ninth goal in 15 appearances for Saints was

added to by Jose Fon Hooiveld and Lallana, wanted to get on the pitch the moment with the fans hard to get off again, but I it. I have always drea playing in the Premier Lea I'm just thankful South believed in me.

"As everyone knows, it's poignant season. I've been every emotion from fru sad, happy – so this tops and I'll enjoy this speci

"It's not just m needed a happy because there are players and staff dressing room who it as much as me. going to be a great ch to pit my wits against and score in the Premier l

For Lallana, who coul followed Theo Walcott, Gar and Alex Oxlade-Chamber of Saints' academy and into time sooner, loyalty reve blissful virtues as he delive final flourish.

At 18, Lallana required surgery for an irregula beat. Now, if you'll exc phrase, he is the he of a side who have f

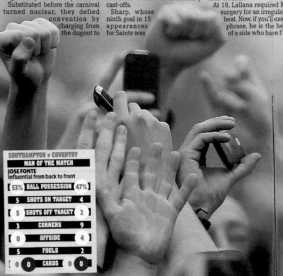

SOUTHAMPTON v COVENTRY
MAN OF THE MATCH
JOSE FONTE
influential from back to front

53%	BALL POSSESSION	47%
5	SHOTS ON TARGET	4
5	SHOTS OFF TARGET	2
3	CORNERS	9
0	OFFSIDE	4
5	FOULS	2
0 0	CARDS	0 0

...HAMPTON 4 COVENTRY 0

Sharp 7 (De Ridder 76). **Goals:** Sharp 16, Fonte 19, Hooiveld 59, Lallana 63, Willis 5 (Henderson 72, 5). **REF:** Anthony Taylor **ATT:** 32,363

...TIFUL SOUTH

...moment for   Sharp to end a season marked with tragedy

Norwich, Manchester City and Watford by winning back-to-back promotions into the top flight.

He said: "I got relegated with the club three years ago and then we were deducted 10 points for being in administration, so it's an incredible feeling to think we're in the best league in the world now.

"I signed a new deal here because I owe the club everything. They gave me a chance, gave me a start and I learned my trade under Alan Pardew (Saints' former manager) and Nigel Adkins came in and he's been fantastic."

Ah, yes – the Adkins diet. The man who spent 10 years as a physio at Scunthorpe before swapping the magic sponge for a magic wand has had four promotion campaigns in five years at the Scun Siro and St Mary's.

Adkins (circled) said: "At the moment I'm probably looking forward most to the fixtures coming out.

"That's when you get excited and start plotting your campaign – the first game of the season, where are we over Christmas, where are we on the last day of the season."

THE PERFECT LIFT
Rickie Lambert is carried off the pitch at a jubilant St Mary's

IT'S HEAVEN SENT
Left: Danny Fox and Sharp celebrate.. while six month ago Sharp (above) was dedicating a goal for Doncaster to his son

JOS WHAT'S NEEDED
Scorer Hooiveld and Guly Do Prado after the Saints went 3-0 up

THORN'S SKY BLUES SHAKE-UP

By MIKE WALTERS

ANDY THORN promised sweeping changes as Coventry bowed out of the Championship like a funeral wake drowned out by a knees-up down the pub.

Sky Blues manager Thorn said: "We need to freshen things up and rebuild in the summer. I've told the players to go away and think about the season – and I don't expect anyone to report back on July 1 feeling sorry for themselves or with a losing mentality.

"Southampton, Norwich, Leicester – they have all gone down to League One and come back stronger."

Acknowledgements

For Tabitha, Max, Grace, Olivia and Amelia. Thanks for all your support.

The author would like to thank:
Richard Havers for his guidance, knowledge and suggestions; Paul Moreton for the opportunity and generous support; David Walker for his ideas and advice; David Scripps, Manjit and the team at Mirrorpix for their invaluable assistance; and all at Haynes Publishing.
Special thanks again to Lawrie McMenemy MBE
Sources: *Match of the Millenium, Dell Diamond, Tie a Yellow Ribbon* (all Hagiology Publishing) and *Saints, A Complete Record of Southampton Football Club 1885-1987* (Breedon Books).
Lastly, to Frank McGhee, Harry Miller, Monte Fresco, Kent Gavin and all those at the *Mirror* who have written about and photographed Hampshire's finest.